Lonely Waters

the diary of a friendship
with E J Moeran

Lionel Hill

Thames Publishing
14 Barlby Road   London W10 6AR

Contents

Illustrations: pages 77–84

Author's note

This book is not intended to be a biography; rather is it an account of the author's friendship with Moeran. The reader will find a brief summary of some of the earlier events in the composer's life on page 115.

The book is dedicated to my friend Stephen Lloyd. My acknowledgements are also due to Geoffrey Stern, Mrs R Jobson, Mrs SK Varley, and especially to Walter Knott (Peers Coetmore's widower) for allowing me access to Moeran's letters to his wife.

Without the help of these friends, and the untiring patience of my wife, the book would not have been possible.

* * * * *

Ernest John Moeran was born on December 31st, 1884, at Isleworth, Middlesex. He spent his childhood in Norfolk, where his father, an Irishman clergyman, held a living.

He was educated at Uppingham Public School and later studied at the Royal College of Music in London.

After serving in the 1914/18 War, during which he received a serious head-wound, he continued his studies with John Ireland.

He came before the public in 1923 with a concert of his works given in London.

After a period of sharing a cottage in Kent with Peter Warlock, he went to live with his aged parents at Kington in Herefordshire. Later he made frequent visits to Kenmare in County Kerry, Eire, a venue which inspired many of his works.

He died at Kenmare on December 1st, 1950, and he is buried in the local churchyard.

To R. Vaughan Williams

LONELY WATERS

E. J. Moeran

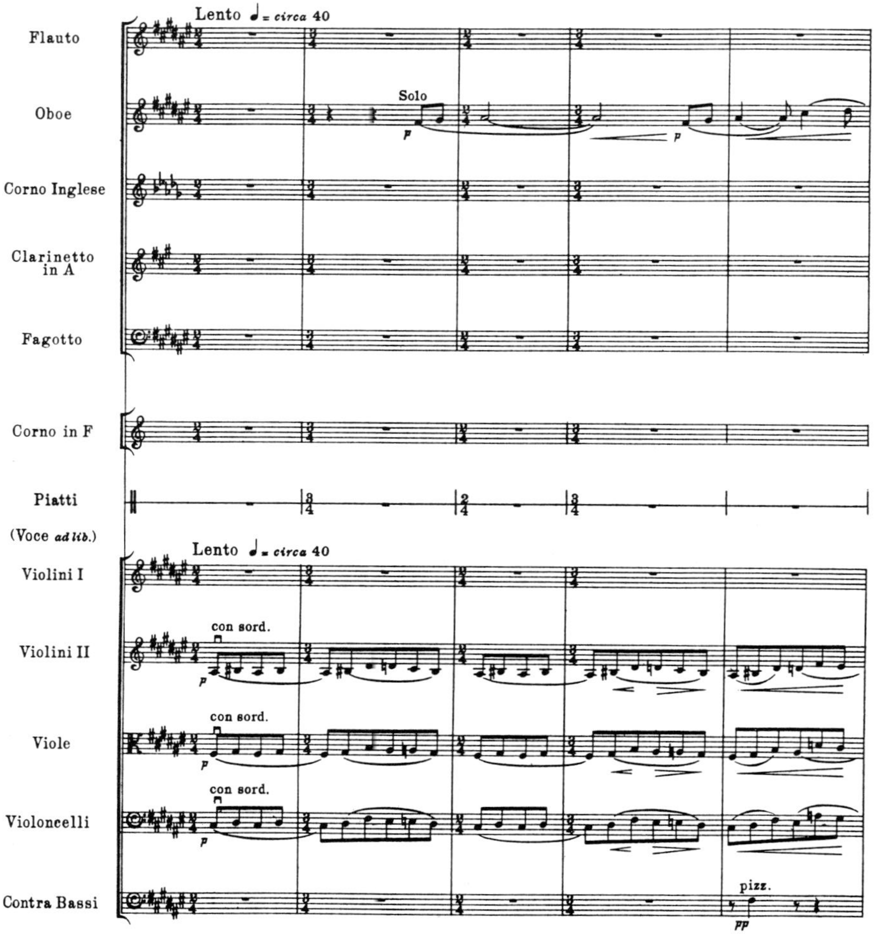

So I'll go down to some lonely waters,
Go down where no one they shall me find,
Where the pretty little small birds do change their voices,
And every moment blow blustering wild.

> *From 'Lonely Waters'* for
> small orchestra and voice,
> by E J Moeran

Jack Moeran as a younger man

Lonely Waters

It all began in 1943 ...

I was in bed awaiting an operation, and happened to switch on the wireless by my bed. My attention was immediately rivetted by the sound coming from the little, old-fashioned set. I could hardly believe my ears, for issuing from that tiny loudspeaker was music shot through with the rare magic of Delius, but with a language of its own.

I had not heard music quite like this before: not since I was fifteen, when I came under the spell of Delius, was I so certain that another composer was about to influence my life.

The piece continued in a leisurely way, pastoral in feeling, and dying away with a voice appearing to call across some lonely expanse of water, the orchestra having faded away some bars previously − surely a folk-song of heart-rending beauty.

Who was this composer? Why had I not heard such compelling music before? Nervously I waited for the announcer's voice in the silence following the final bars.

'You have been listening to *Lonely Waters* by E J Moeran', it said. Surely a perfect description of the music's message!

Several weeks elapsed − operation and convalescence − and still the haunting loveliness of this piece remained with me. It was obviously by a British composer with a deep feeling for Nature, and I was pretty sure that he was a contemporary.

I had written to Delius shortly before his death in 1934, asking him to autograph a score of mine, and had received back not only the score, charmingly inscribed, but also a kind letter; and now the time had come to make every effort, once again, to make contact with a mind so in tune with my own. It was something that had to be done, but how?

After much thought, my wife and I decided to write to an old acquaintance, Gerald Moore, the accompanist. Our letter brought a prompt reply: yes, Gerald did know Moeran and had in fact played his Violin Sonata − 'A fine work' − and suggested that we write to the BBC for his address. This I did without delay, and received the information required. It seemed that Moeran lived at Kington in Herefordshire, close to the Welsh mountains.

9

In my first letter, dated April 10th, 1943, I said how much his music meant to me, and was curious to know whether he liked Delius, as one sensed a similar feeling at times. As the days passed I waited impatiently, for would he bother to answer?

I was cutting the lawn at Woodfield, our home in Bucks, a few weeks later when a letter arrived with a Hereford postmark. This must be it! A second later I was holding open the first letter of what was to be a voluminous correspondence that would last until his death seven years later. It was dated April 13th 1943.

The letter began with apologies for delay in replying, 'As I am at the moment convalescent from having been ill, but I will do so when I am a bit better'.

This brief reply to my long letter gave me more pleasure than I can express. Even now, all these years later, I can still feel the thrill of holding that letter in my hands. Evidently he was going to write again, so perhaps he would answer some of my queries.

He certainly did, for on April 21st there arrived a long letter of much interest:

Dear Mr. Hill,
I am now better again, and take the opportunity of writing to you at greater length.

I have always had a great admiration for Delius, that is to say what I call good Delius. There is also some very bad Delius, and I have grave suspicions of the musical perceptibility of those who, no doubt with laudable intentions, perform such works as his second violin sonata, cello sonata and his piano music. Some of his later orchestral music is extremely poor, notably the *Song before Sunrise*, and the *Second Dance Rhapsody*. In fact he seems to have gone to pieces roughly from 1913 or so to the end of his life. It may have been a subconscious forboding of his illness, or else he had just written himself out and run dry, so to speak.

But it always seems to me that it is doing a colossal disservice to Delius to perform and, what is worse still, to record these later works at all.

However, my love of his really great works remains unimpaired by the trash he wrote latterly. To my mind the *Mass of Life, Songs of Sunset, Sea Drift, Village Romeo and Juliet, First Dance Rhapsody*, most of *Brigg Fair*, and the *Song of the High Hills* are masterpieces, each in its own different way.

The other published opera, performed in Germany but never here so far, *Fennimore and Gerda*, I don't know, but I have heard good accounts of it from those who do.

10

I should also have added *Appalachia* to the list of great works.

My first introduction to Delius was in 1913, when I was a student at the R.C.M. and I heard his Piano Concerto at a Balfour Gardiner concert at the Queen's Hall. I shall never forget the profound impression it made on me at the time, also the lordly and superior comments on it by some of my fellow students.

You mentioned the *New Statesman* with regard to myself. I never read this paper; it always seems to me precious in its outlook on life; I have been told that Sackville West rarely misses an opportunity of having a hit at me. However, as I never read any criticisms at all of my work unless they happen to occur in whatever newspaper I light on for other news after a concert, it really doesn't matter to me in the least. I am sorry you couldn't get *Stalham River* at Boosey and Hawkes. It is to be had at Chesters. I have not a copy of it, but I am sending you its companion piece, incidentally a much better one I think.

I seem to have lost the knack of writing piano music recently. It may be that my grand piano is parked at a relative's house for the duration, and I have to use a particularly foul upright for my work.

I am struggling to finish a *Rhapsody* for piano and orchestra in time for the Proms. The piano part is written, thank Heaven, and I am now on the congenial task of making a full score.

I hope we may meet some day.

Yours sincerely,
E.J. Moeran

I have quoted this letter in full, partly because it was the first of many, but also because the contents are of great interest. One could sense that the writer was a friendly man. My feeling that he admired Delius was confirmed, though his damning remarks about certain works came as a surprise, and I could not agree with them, especially with regard to the Cello Sonata. As our friendship developed, however, he was to reconsider many of these opinions and in particular came to admire much the Cello Sonata, as I will show later.

It has always been an enigma to me that he so loved Delius' Piano Concerto, which is generally agreed to be one of the latter's least typical works. He was to hold this opinion to the end.

In my letter I had condemned a derogatory article in the *New Statesman* by Edward Sackville West, and Moeran's comments on this and critiques in general were, as I came to learn, typical of the man.

With his letter came a piano piece published by Chester called *Toccata*, an early composition of 1923 and very typical of his work at that period. It has been used as a high-grade test piece at the RCM.

Moeran's comments on the piano *Rhapsody* are revealing. The piano part of this work and of the later Cello Sonata were all, except for a few songs, that he was to write for the instrument. There is no doubt that his great love was for the orchestra, which he thoroughly understood.

However, not to digress further at this point, I was delighted and intrigued by this first letter and felt that I must keep up the correspondance, so I wrote again within a few days and received the following reply:

April 30th, 1943.
Dear Mr. Hill,
Many thanks for your letter of April 28th. and for your kindness in telling me that you keep 'Open house'. Unfortunately, in these days of petrol rationing it is very unlikely I should be in your district. Where is Seer Green? However, I hope I may see you at the Proms later on. Delius' Violin Concerto is full of superb things, but it contains one section − the 6/8 dance section near the end − which I find lets the work down.

I think *Eventyr* is good, but not his top-notch. *Cynara*, I regret to say, I am unacquainted with. In my previous list I forgot to mention the wonderful piece *Paris*, one of his very finest achievements. I am not sure either whether I included *Appalachia*, which again I think is a great work − a really great work.

Do listen to Vaughan Williams' *Flos Campi* on Sunday, to my mind it is one of the outstanding works by any living composer.

So you are Albert Sammons' son-in-law! You must be some relation by marriage or otherwise to my old friend Ethel Hobday.
Yours sincerely,
E.J. Moeran
P.S. Wouldn't a four-handed arrangement perhaps be easier to do for my Symphony? However, perhaps you lack a partner to play it with.
P.P.S. *In a Summer Garden* is, I think, one of Delius' most satisfactory pieces also.

These fascinating comments on Delius, my favourite composer, by another composer who I felt would gain my affection on closer acquaintance, brought pleasure of a very special kind. One sensed that both were motivated by a love of Nature and events of long ago. The last movement of Moeran's Violin Concerto provoked the same nostalgia to be found so profusely in Delius. I was yet to learn of other influences on Moeran, but none was to eradicate this first impression on me.

Some days later came another letter:

Kington,
Herefordshire.
June 12th 1943.

Dear Mr. Hill,

I found your letter here on my return from Arran Island this week.

You must forgive me for brevity, but I am very busy.

There is no complete list of my published works. However, there are piano works (early) at Schott's, Augener's and the Oxford Press; songs at Boosey & Hawkes; Novello, Oxford Press, Curwen's and Augener's. This includes part-songs, songs for mixed voices and some folk-song arrangements.

You also ask about church music: I have a *Te Deum* and *Jubilate* at the Oxford Press; this is frequently to be heard on Sundays in cathedrals. Both Westminster Abbey and Southwark do it from time to time.

There is also a *Magnificat* and *Nunc Dimittis* (temporarily out of print) at the Oxford Press, and an anthem, *Praise the Lord, O Jerusalem*. Another short unaccompanied anthem is at Novello, the title of which I forget.

There is chamber music at Oxford Press (Piano Trio, broadcast last Tuesday), Chester (Violin Sonata & String Quartet), Augener (String Trio, miniature score) and Boosey & Hawkes (Sonata for two violins).

Hawkes publish a full score of my 1st Rhapsody, and Oxford Press *In the Mountain Country*, symphonic impression for orchestra. Full scores of *Lonely Waters* and *Whythorne's Shadow* are at Novello, also the vocal scores of *Nocturne, Songs of Springtime* and a recent work, *Phyllida and Corydon*.

That, I think, is about the lot. The new *Rhapsody* for piano and orchestra is being published by Chester; it is hoped to have it on sale before the first performance in August.

I am sorry you don't like Mozart. To me he is supreme in some respects. Surely you must like Bach's 48 preludes and fugues and the great organ works even, if like myself, you are bored with his gebrauchsmusik such as many of the concerti, suites etc. The promenade concert type of Bach is usually bad Bach. The early Beethoven quartets, violin sonatas and parts of the piano sonatas are very fine to my way of thinking and what about the septet? As there is such Wagnerian influence in Delius, I am surprised you rule him out. I think both *Tristan* and *Meistersinger* are masterpieces. I must stop now, as I want to listen-in to another masterpiece, about which you may agree, namely Schubert's Octet.

E.J.M.

Curiously, he does not mention the G minor Symphony or Violin Concerto among his published works, both published by Novello.

13

In after years we were to discuss our opinions on various composers, agreeing most of the time — for instance our dislike of Schumann, most of Britten, and indifference to Liszt. More about his musical tastes appear in his next letter:

> Kington,
> June 16th 1943.
>
> Dear Mr. Hill,
>
> I suggest your getting Mosco Carner's little book, the title of which I forget, but I think it may be *Modern Harmony*.
>
> I do not see anything in the Atonalists such as Webern, Krenek and company. They have just merely succeeded in inventing a new branch of academism, more circumscribed than the old counterpoint of Palestrina. I am much moved by some of Bartok's work. Don't bracket him with Webern. Bartok is not an Atonalist. I have just bought and am studying his Op. 7 Quartet with score and records; it is full of grand music. I am surprised that Britten's *St. Cecilia* is recorded. I think it very poor stuff, but I admire the *Sinfonia da Requiem*, and certain of his things.
>
> Of music in an entirely different idiom, I have been getting pleasure out of Roussel's G minor Symphony. This record and the Bartok I bought cheap at a sale at Hereford, together with other records.
>
> I hope I may meet you at a Prom in July.
>
> Yours sincerely,
> E.J. Moeran
>
> P.S. I also got records of Stravinsky's *Symphony of Psalms*, some of which is magnificent.

To me, at that time, these musical opinions were most satisfying, and further confirmed the similarity of our tastes. His dislike of the atonalists was a great relief. At a later stage we were to discuss Britten at length, and agree that there was something in his music which repelled us.

* * * * *

There now occurs a gap in our correspondence of more than two months, but during this period occurred two important events. Moeran's Violin Concerto was down for performance at a Prom on July 30th, the soloist being Arthur Catterall, to whom the work is dedicated. We went to hear this lovely piece, whose Celtic nostalgia is so poignant.

14

I remember thinking how my father-in-law, Albert Sammons, would wring the utmost from this score. As we shall see, this idea was to materialise a few years later.

When the concert was over we decided to take our courage in both hands and go and look for Moeran. So we made for the Artists' Room and stood nervously in the corridor, looking for someone of whose appearance we had not the slightest knowledge. It was not long before I spotted a man of slightly over-medium height slowly walking in our direction. He was dressed in country tweeds and carried a walking stick. His broad face was of a rubicund complexion which suited the brushed-back grey hair.

As he approached us I said to my wife 'This is Moeran, I'm sure', and went up to him, saying 'Excuse me, are you by any chance Mr Moeran?' He looked at me with rather blood-shot eyes and said, without hesitation, 'You must be Lionel Hill?'

It was a wonderful moment. We discussed the performance of the Violin Concerto we had just heard, and I asked him how long he intended to stay in town; I felt instinctively that he was a countryman by nature, and would not prolong his visit to London. His vague reply prompted me to suggest that he should come to stay with us. He looked so pleased at this idea that we both almost shouted 'Why not come back with us tonight!' He replied that he couldn't on this occasion, but would love to do so after the first performance of the piano *Rhapsody* on August 19th.

The next few weeks passed agonisingly slowly, but at last the great day arrived and we entered the Albert Hall beside ourselves with excitement. The programme contained works by Elgar, Granville Bantock, Moeran, Tchaikovsky and Beethoven, and the soloists were Mary Jarred and Harriet Cohen. Sir Adrian Boult conducted the BBC Orchestra.

I waited impatiently until at last Miss Cohen entered to applause and sat down at the piano, adjusted her stool, looked at the conductor – and the *Rhapsody* sprang to life.

I had studied the piano reduction score of this work during previous weeks; nevertheless, I was captivated by the triple-time entry of the cellos and double basses, followed by the piano's dramatic statement of the first theme, and as the performance continued I became enthralled by the spell that this composer could weave. There was a juxtaposition of violence and lyricism that I was later to know was typical of the

15

man himself. There was also a pervading sense of nostalgia for the pastoral scene of long ago − something whose roots lay deeper than folk music itself.

After the concert Moeran suggested that we go to see Harriet Cohen in the Artists' Room and ask her to autograph my score, which she graciously did. The three of us then left the hall and made our way, in the blackout, to Marylebone Station, where we caught a train for Seer Green Halt in Buckinghamshire − for our house, Woodfield, lay in a secluded part of this lovely county.

I don't think we spoke much on the journey, for in those war-time days there was complete darkness in every compartment and most passengers dozed the time away.

When we arrived at Seer Green we stepped on to the platform in utter blackness. This little halt was originally built to serve Beaconsfield Golf Club, the clubhouse of which stood about 150 yards away. The Great Central tank engine puffed and chugged its way towards Beaconsfield, its next stop, and we stood in complete gloom and eerie silence. I remember Moeran gratefully inhaling the fresh Bucks air and knocking out his pipe on his upturned heel.

As we walked down the dark lane bordered by tall trees, through the narrow bridge over which our train had just passed, I reflected on the amazing circumstances that had brought the three of us together in the heart of the country on a pitch-black night, and that this spell-binding composer was actually to be our guest.

I had designed and built the house we were approaching at the time of our marriage in 1931. It was of brick and tile with four bedrooms, two bathrooms, kitchen, and one large living-room 28′ by 18′. The garden was on a slope and included a wooded dell. Regarded from the front the house seemed isolated, as indeed it was, there being nothing but a large field between it and the railway, which was just emerging from a cutting at this point. To the left, and barely visible through a thick, high hedge, was our only neighbour, a low brick house some distance away. I was certain that daylight would bring the perfect setting for Moeran and his music.

On entering the house his first act was to go into the living room and change into house slippers. Straightening himself he remarked on the pleasant room and especially the heavy oak beams. He then suddenly said 'My God, how that woman *digs*!' 'What do you mean?'

I said. 'Harriet Cohen, of course,' he replied, and I knew what he meant.

At bedtime we showed Moeran to his room, and retired for the night, going over and over all that had happened during that memorable day.

* * * * *

Moeran's first visit lasted a day or two. We took him for several long walks, which he much enjoyed. He always used a walking stick, for he had a 'gammy' leg which he said was due to 'an accident with a rowing boat'. He and I were a pair in that respect as I also carried a stick at that time, the result of a motor-cycle accident three years previously.

During his first stay with us we soon came to know and appreciate this curious man. Firstly, his reserved friendliness. He seldom laughed outright, but his slow smile revealed an inner mirth that was most infectious. His complete lack of self-importance was soon evident, and I was to learn that he loathed pomposity in man or music. He was a constant pipe-smoker, another trait we had in common, but he seldom smoked whilst on a country walk. He said it took away the fragrance of natural smells!

Our house was situated near Jordans Village, founded by the Quakers to be adjacent to the Friends' Meeting House, where William Penn and his family are buried. The village consists of a large green surrounded by pretty cottages, and the approach lay through Crutches Wood, a thick plantation of beech trees.

Out for a walk during this first visit, I took Moeran up to this village. He made some small purchases at the local stores, outside which was a telephone kiosk, when he suddenly said 'I must phone Ralph Hill about meeting him in town,' and entered the kiosk, where I could see him impatiently fumbling with coins.

Ralph Hill was a distinguished music critic of the period. I don't know if Moeran got any satisfaction from that call, but he emerged with that slight smile we were beginning to know so well, and as we strolled over the village green he turned towards me and said 'Call me Jack — all my orchestral friends do'.

From that moment he was Jack to us all.

My diary tells me that during this visit we listened on the wireless

17

to Delius' *Sea Drift*. This must have given us both great pleasure, for it was a work we held in high esteem.

On the day of his departure we went up by train to Marylebone, walking across Dorset Square to Baker Street Station, and stopping half-way to visit Webster & Girling, the ticket agents, who also had a gramophone record department in the basement where I had bought most of my records, including works by Moeran. I introduced him to my friends behind the counter, who were delighted and flattered by Jack's courteousness.

* * * * *

It was at this time that I learnt of Jack's great and abiding love of steam engines and everything concerning railways. The fact that we lived within sight and sound of this passion made his visit to us all the more enjoyable. His knowledge of railway timetables was prodigious, and many times at breakfast or lunch he would suddenly say 'Sshh', and sit bolt upright with head cocked and almost shout 'Here comes the 10.30 Birkenhead express!' Glancing at his watch, he would continue with excitement 'She's got a Castle loco on today, probably the Aberdovey Castle,' and jumping up he would rush upstairs to the far bedroom, from which a good view of passing trains could be obtained. A few minutes later down he came with a happy self-satisfied expression and say 'It was the Aberdovey alright!' and continue his meal in silence.

The first time this odd behaviour occurred we all sat in stunned silence for a while. It was a new experience for our family, and greatly amused Judy and Nicholas, our children aged ten and seven at this time.

On many future occasions I was to be astonished by Jack's uncanny knowledge of the age of steam. For instance, we might be awaiting a train at Seer Green Halt and hear, but not yet see, an express approaching in the far distance, causing Jack to strain his ears for a moment and then remark casually 'Here comes a Hall class loco,' and when the train roared past, sure enough it was. When I asked him how he knew such things he replied 'By the beat of the engine; every engine is an individual with its own sound.' Even now I still marvel at his knowledge of those wonderful days of steam, and those who knew Jack will always hear in his music, at certain times, the echoes of his passion for railways, especially so in the Symphony in G minor.

18

The days following Jack's departure seemed curiously empty. But there arrived a letter in his handwriting addressed to my wife:

August 30th

Dear Betty,

I did not arrive home until yesterday morning, very tired after a most strenuous three days in London, topped up with an all-night journey.

All sorts of things cropped up, including a long session with Walter Legge at the Gramophone place in Abbey Road. He lives very near you, and he was so sorry I did not know it, as he says he was at home at a loose end last Sunday and wishes we could all have foregathered.

He hopes that if you will have me to stay again for a week-end on some future occasion, that we can meet, as he would like to know you and Lionel. He says that he made the Grieg records with the Budapest Quartet seven days before the War started, but saved them up for publication against the date of the Grieg Centenary.

I see in my Saturday *Telegraph* that Delius' *Mass of Life* is down for performance at Albert Hall on May 13th. − mirabile dictu, Nietsche in war-time!!

Yours sincerely,

Jack Moeran

P.S. Thank you again for such an exceptionally happy and enjoyable stay at Jordans.

We were glad to learn that Jack's first stay with us had been a success, and felt that we need not hesitate to invite him again.

In early September I wrote to Jack, enclosing the current copy of *The Gramophone* magazine, the founder and editor of which was Compton MacKenzie the novelist. For some long while I had been at the centre of a correspondence in this paper on the pros and cons of Delius, and the present number contained a particularly violent diatribe against this composer.

Jack's answer, as expected, was much to the point:

September 10th

Dear Lionel,

Thanks for sending *The Gramophone*. I will return it and other earlier numbers to you, so that you will have them complete. I like MacKenzie's editorial in the current issue. As for the letter on the Delius question, I do know that there are people who feel like that about him. I think it is largely because they have originally approached him, or else have been introduced to him, via his poorer works, e.g. this chap quotes *A Song before Sunrise* and I am bound to say I agree with him there. He may not know the *Mass of Life, Songs of Sunset, First Dance Rhapsody, Village Romeo and Juliet* — that is to say four of Delius' best works which are unrecorded, barring *The Paradise Garden* intermezzo.

I saw Cecil Gray after leaving you that week-end. I asked him about *Fennimore*; he knows it well, he says, but he does not consider much of it to be good Delius. Still, I should like to see it.

I am engaged to broadcast from Dublin on October 15th. I shall have to visit London before the end of September to see about my travel permit to Eire. If it would not put you out, Betty also, to have me for a short week-end, I would suggest that we might make a date together with Walter Legge.

I shall in all probability stay in Eire for a bit after the broadcast.

I am very interested to hear your opinion of Iris Loveridge. She and a violinist are to play my fiddle sonata on October 25th. I believe it is to be at Wigmore Hall.

She seems to be a singularly intelligent girl, blessed, too, with a decided sense of humour. Such people are excellent to work with, and I found her so musical that there was very little to tell her about the Variations. I took her the *Rhapsody* on the same occasion, and she started reading at sight the more difficult parts with no trouble at all.

Yours,
Jack Moeran

I had been to hear Iris Loveridge play at the Wigmore Hall only recently, but my memory fails me as to her programme, which must have included some work by Jack or I would not have gone.

Also during this period Miss Loveridge came down from London to study with Jack certain of his piano pieces, which she was to play in public later on. Jack, of course, was staying with us. He and I met her at the station and conducted her to our house, where she and Jack were left to work in seclusion.

Betty and I were thrilled to hear Jack's music being played with such authority, and when we judged that the session was coming to an end we quietly entered the room. Jack was standing beside the seated pianist, his face flushed with the nervous strain he had just undergone. Without warning he strode to the fireplace, snatched some letters from the mantelpiece and announced brusquely 'I must go to the post', and, banging the front door behind him, left the three of us aghast and not a little amused!

When he returned in a more relaxed mood we all had tea, and were sorry to say goodbye to Miss Loveridge for she had proved to be a very pleasant person.

For the rest of the day Jack exuded bonhommie and when, after supper, he sat down at the piano and explored my scores, it gave me the utmost pleasure to hear his comments on some of my favourite music. For example, he was surprised and delighted by Grieg's Opus 66 arrangements of Norwegian folk-tunes, which he had not heard before, and remarked on their apt and daring harmony, especially *In Ola Valley*, which Delius had also used in *On Hearing the First Cuckoo in Spring*.

Jack was an indifferent pianist, certainly at the time I knew him, but he could at least give a good idea of his own music. In any case our piano was a poor sample of the upright variety. Sometimes Jack would get a piece really going when a key would stick down, whereupon panic stations took over. Repeatedly hitting the offending note and shouting 'Play, damn you, – PLAY!', he would almost exhaust himself in baffled annoyance.

In view of Jack's wish to meet Walter Legge, I wrote to the latter soon after the events described above, and suggested a meeting which was arranged for September 24th. Jack came for a few days, during which we three met at 'The Cricketers' pub in Seer Green, about ten minutes' walk from our house. I remember that on the way Jack said 'I don't think you'll care much for this chap; I don't, but one can't choose in these matters and he is pretty influential, and I think he is going to commission a work from me for ENSA.' Legge was indeed in charge of music for the Armed Forces, so I saw what Jack meant.

We found Legge at the pub. He had come over from a neighbouring village. After introductions we took our drinks to a table by the bay window, which commanded a pretty view across the old churchyard.

Legge told Jack that he was about to ask several British composers to produce short works suitable for entertaining the Forces at ENSA concerts, and suggested that an overture lasting not more than ten minutes would fit the bill. Further, it must be for a Mozart-sized orchestra, with single woodwind and two French horns, etc.

I wondered what Jack's reaction to such a commission would be, because on a previous occasion I had asked him why he had never written a film score. His reply was that he could not compose to order – which was a pity, for his evocative music would have enhanced certain types of film. I reminded Jack that his teacher, John Ireland, had written a fine score for the film *The Overlanders*, and Jack's music would have provided atmosphere (witness the recent use of his scores in the TV series 'The Onedin Line').

In this instance, however, I could see that he was pleased with Legge's suggestion and we said goodbye in the best of spirits. The outcome of this commission was *An Overture for a Masque*, which received its first performance the following year.

It was about this time that I took my first photo of Jack — walking along the railway bank over the deep cutting previously mentioned. I shall always treasure this, for in it he looks so well and in his prime, compared with later studio portraits.

A passing German bomber jettisoned its bombs around Beaconsfield and district the night before Jack's visit. The next morning the milkman gleefully announced that one of them had dropped in a field between Jordans and Seer Green. No sooner had Jack learnt this exciting piece of news than he was impatient to go and inspect the crater. So he donned his tweed overcoat and peaked cap, his usual attire for country walks, and we set out across the fields. We eventually found the site and inspected the enormous hole, which fascinated Jack, who loved anything out of the ordinary.

* * * * *

In view of the large part that gramophone records played in our friendship, I must pause to explain that since early childhood I had been a keen collector of gramophone records, which numbered several hundred when Jack first came to stay with us. In the early days of the war I became the proud owner of an acoustic machine with an enormous papier-mâché horn shaped like a swan's neck, which grew from 2″ at the tone arm to 36″ in diameter at the bell-like opening. One used fibre needles in the specially tuned soundbox, and this instrument was capable of producing a mellow sound of great naturalness, especially in chamber music and voices. Indeed, I think that it dealt with strings more faithfully than modern so-called hi-fi. The long-playing record sounded the death knell to this marvellous machine. At any rate, for the next four years Jack and I did all our listening to this gramophone, which was a constant source of joy to us.

In those happy days of his visits he would often ask to hear my records, most of which were to his taste; but by far his favourites were the 3 volumes of the Delius Society issues. These came out between 1934 – 1938 and contained such works as *Sea Drift, Appalachia, Paris,* etc, all of which gave Jack much pleasure.

There was also an excerpt from *Fennimore and Gerda*, an *Intermezzo*, with a ravishing oboe solo by Leon Goossens, prince of players on this instrument. Jack adored this piece. No matter what our musical fare had been on those long evening sessions with the gramophone, he often said 'We can't go to bed without hearing that marvellous Goossens piece'. Whenever I play the whole opera, now available on long-play records, it is the 'Goossens piece' which so clearly brings to mind those far-off happy times spent in the company of my two favourite composers. Could this experience have prompted Jack to write his Oboe Quartet for Goossens within the next few years?

Jack left us on September 28th, leaving his hosts in the usual state of nervous exhaustion they had now come to expect. His companionship was so vital, and every moment so interesting, that his absence always left a void.

Complete silence followed until October 27th, when a postcard arrived: –

> Cahirciveen,
> Co. Kerry.
> Here you see a picture of our local railway, with the mountain Knocknadoler in the background. Everything here is as inspiring as ever, even more so than usual.
> E.J.M.

A previous postcard, which, although not of significance, does show one facet of his sense of humour:

> Llandrindod Wells,
> September 16th, 1943.
> Thanks for your letter. I am over here today, Heavens knows why! A most depressing place consisting of hotel, private ditto:, and boarding houses with names such as Chatsworth, Southlea, Ferncliffe, Sunny Bank, etc.
> E.J.M.

On November 7th Jack arrived unexpectedly for two nights, he said, but stayed five! The time was spent in going for walks and listening to records, with bouts at the piano. During his stay we went up to London to see Boosey & Hawkes about publication of one of his scores. We then went to a concert, and Cecil Gray, the author and composer, joined us. Jack came back with me for the night and left the next day.

On November 18th I had lunch with him in town by previous phone appointment and met Peers Coetmore, the cellist, for the first time. She was later to become his wife.

We received the following letter a few days after this event, addressed to my wife:

> Kington,
> Herefordshire
>
> Dear Betty,
>
> Here I am again on the Welsh border. I put my head out of the window passing through Seer Green yesterday on the 4.5 pm. express from Paddington, in case I should see either of the children running about. I know Nicholas has a friend in the signal box, and I thought there might be a bare chance of his pottering about there.
>
> I finished the Clare Delius book about her brother; it is full of inaccuracies, some of them even amounting to the status of howler. I will bring it back to London next week.
>
> Also, we have heaps of eggs here, and to spare, so I will re-imburse you with regard to your generous action in supplying me with eggs to take with me to London.
>
> I expect to go to town next week from Thursday to Monday. If you could put up with me, I would love to run down just for one night, as I don't expect to budge again from here before mid-January.
>
> Again, thank you so much for your kind hospitality. I always enjoy every minute of my time in your house.
>
> Yours sincerely,
> Jack

This intended visit did not materialize.

On November 28th, Jack rang me up at my office, and the following day we had lunch together at a little restaurant in the Finchley Road, during which Peers joined us.

A month elapsed before his next letter, which contained both sad and interesting news:

24

Kington,
Herefordshire
20/12/43

My dear Lionel,

Thanks for your letter. I am afraid you must think me remiss in being out of touch with you, but there has been a succession of events which have over-shadowed everything else. First of all, I arrived at Stanmore three weeks ago, I think it was, last Saturday; and found Catterall dying. As you know, he died on the Sunday morning and I did not know even previously that he was ill. The family had been trying to contact me in Eire, thinking I was still over there. His funeral was not until the following Thursday and I have been taken up with affairs concerning the Catteralls meanwhile.

Then I had an S.O.S. from here that my father was seriously ill, and had to come down here again. He had acute bronchitis but made a wonderful rally, so much so that I returned to London. I came back here last Wednesday. My father, I am sorry to tell you, had a relapse during the middle of last week. He died very peacefully on Saturday evening. Pneumonia had set in and at his age, 85, there was no hope of his recovery.

It is really as well, though, for had he lived it would have been only to eke out a miserable existence for the remainder of his life as a practically helpless invalid, as the illness of the past three months had so irreparably weakened him.

I am glad to hear that Albert Sammons is having a go at my Concerto. You know the story of this work: how originally I wanted to show it to him, only that the matter did not rest entirely in my hands. If it is ever going to be recorded I sincerely hope that it should be he, and nobody else, who should be asked to do it.

The last time you and I met was at lunch at the 'Winchester' with Peers Coetmore. She and I are in the process of becoming engaged to each other, although I cannot be sure now exactly what date our regard for each other culminated in a definite engagement to be married. But there it is now; she went away last Saturday week for her six months tour of the Middle East, and we propose being married very soon after her return. This engagement gave my poor father the most wonderful comfort during his last illness. He was so fond of Peers, and my mother has since told me that when she was down here playing and stayed in our house in September he said 'I do wish those two could take a fancy to each other', meaning Peers and myself.

I hope to be Londonwards about the end of January. Perhaps you can put me up for a day or two then.

A Happy Christmas to you all,
Jack

The death of Arthur Catterall must have been a severe blow to Jack, for although he had previously told me that he had Sammons in mind while writing the Violin Concerto, he had nevertheless the benefit of Catterall's first performance, and indeed the work is dedicated to this fine player.

Jack was one of those people who bottle up their emotions, but I well remember his sadness at the death of his father.

At the time of this letter my family had not met Jack's fiancée, though I had done so on two occasions. She had struck me as a jolly, rather tomboyish person, with a direct, outspoken manner. Jack was obviously pleased with the whole situation and so, therefore, was I, but neither of us could have known what was to be the outcome of his alliance.

I mentioned in my previous letter that I had persuaded my father-in-law to look over the Violin Concerto. This is the way it happened:

Albert was staying with us and whilst on a walk through the glorious beechwoods that stood around our valley I said to him, 'Do you know any of E. J. Moeran's music, Albert?' He replied, 'I've heard of him but can't say I know any of his music.'

'Well honestly,' I replied, 'he's written a superb Violin Concerto which is right up your street. Some of it has the feeling of Delius, and I'm absolutely certain its for you, and you alone. Do please try it over'.

After a short silence Albert said, 'I'm very wary of learning a new modern work after my experience with the Bloch Concerto.' He paused and said, 'After all the trouble I took to learn that difficult work, there was only one performance. In any case, I'm thinking of retiring from the concert platform, and will just keep up my teaching at the RCM'.

This was a blow, but I left the subject alone for a while and waited for another opportunity, which luckily came before Albert returned to London, and as a result of much persuasion he agreed to look over the concerto.

In retrospect I seem to have involved Sammons in the performance of two concertos at a time when he was not looking for engagements of this nature. Columbia had asked him to record the Delius Concerto with Malcolm Sargent and the Liverpool Philharmonic Orchestra, and this was completed in 1944. The project was the result of the many letters I was able to send to Columbia, these being in answer to my plea in *The Gramophone* for a recording of this work. These letters had come from all over the world, many from men serving in the Forces, and also led to a recording of Delius' Third Violin Sonata by Decca, the artists being Sammons and Kathleen Long.

These '78' records of the Concerto have now been re-issued on an LP with a greatly improved sound spectrum.

Albert was staying with us when the concerto was recorded and had to go up to Liverpool for the session. On his return his first words were, 'It won't be any good, old boy. Walter Legge was in charge of the recording and he kept interrupting and shouting, "You're too near the mike, Albert, − − back, BACK!"'

Albert was correct, for when the records were issued it was only too evident that his beautiful performance was overpowered by the orchestra. However, this fault has largely been put right on the recent transfer to a long-playing record. I do wish that Jack could have heard this, as he so loved the original, with all its faults.

Before I could write and let him know that Albert had consented to try the concerto, I received the following letter:

December 27th

Dear Lionel,

Have you any news of Albert Sammons, as to whether he likes my Concerto well enough to take it up?

The point is that (and this is in strict confidence) I heard from Bliss to the effect that the B.B.C. Symphony Orchestra intend doing it at headquarters, and I wonder if I might go so far as to suggest that Albert be asked to play it.

Moreover, it still awaits performance in the North, where my Symphony is at the moment going the rounds since its publication.

The point is that if Albert learns it there should be opportunities for several performances. N.B. It was the only novelty of the 1942 Proms Season that was repeated this year, not only in the Prom. Season, but played at the Royal Philharmonic Society as well. So it might even stick in the repertory, and Albert Sammons is the only living violinist I would like to have interpret it.

Yours,

Jack

Sir Arthur Bliss was a very influential person at this time. Jack had told me that when he suggested, prior to Catterall's first performance, that the Concerto be offered to Sammons, Bliss had abruptly replied, 'Think yourself lucky to get a performance at all.'

'And that was that,' said Jack. 'The matter was out of my hands.'

Bliss was not among the English composers whom Jack discussed with me, and I don't think there was mutual attraction.

27

Within 24 hours another letter lay on our doormat. It was dated December 28th:

Dear Lionel,

Thank you all at Woodfield for the Christmas present of *Appalachia*, which arrived this morning. I am delighted to have the score of this masterpiece. I had already written about getting the records of this, and of the *Sea Drift* album.

I am interested that you were bitten with some Bach. I cannot recall the particular movement which appealed so much to you. Look out for a chance of hearing Brandenburg Concerto No. 6; the slow movement of that is superb. So is the whole work, but the Brandenburg Concerti are only good in parts. I still plump for many of the 48 Preludes & Fugues. The Passacaglia in C minor for organ is a very great work, and is, to my mind, wonderfully enhanced in Respighi's orchestral transcription.

I was only able to hear the first movement of Sammons and Moore in the Ireland No. 2 last night. Those two make an ideal combination for sonata playing. The Ireland sonata, I find, wears very well.

Best wishes to you all for 1944.

Yours ever,

Jack Moeran

P.S. I sent you by way of a Christmas card a composition by old 'Beaker'. I hope it arrived.

The Brandenburg Concerto I referred to was the No. 4. The John Ireland Violin Sonata No. 2 was first performed by Sammons in 1917 and is dedicated to him. The Sonata was a huge success and made Ireland famous overnight.

Jack's postscript reference to 'Old Beaker' can only be explained by a slight diversion. Jack was educated at Uppingham Public School, and I at Clifton College, near Bristol. We often used to compare stories about our lives spent at boarding school at the beginning of this century. 'Old Beaker' (C S Lang) was one of the music masters at Clifton in my day, and was in fact my piano teacher. He was a very fine organist, and was later to become well-known in the world outside the cloisters. He had been a contemporary of Jack's at the Royal College of Music, where both became pupils of Stanford, and was known even then as 'Beaker'. Jack loved to re-call how 'Beaker', who hero-worshipped Stanford, would follow the great man all over the College, hands clasped behind him under his gown and mimicking every gesture made by The Master. Jack also could mime all this to perfection.

28

The composition by 'Beaker' did arrive safely, and turned out to be a short piece for choir and organ.

* * * * *

Before continuing the story of our friendship with Jack Moeran, I must pause to sum up our impressions of this lovable, and at times unpredictable man. The past eight months had been a hectic time for my family. Jack's many visits, usually of two or more days' duration, always kept us on our toes. Although he had become one of the family, and was less trouble than most visitors, his very presence was so stimulating that his departure usually left us in a state of lassitude.

He had a great sense of humour and a special gift of mimicry, which was never cruel but extremely funny. He was quick to notice anything odd or unusual about someone and would, in the most kindly way, 'take' him or her off. For instance, he might point to someone and whisper, 'I say, do you think that chap over there knows that one of his ears sticks out at rightangles?'

Another of Jack's traits that only gradually became apparent was his fondness for the 'hard stuff'. At our very first meeting, at the Albert Hall, we noticed his flushed complexion and somewhat dazed eyes. I could now look back and realize that he must have just emerged from the bar suitably fortified. I will have more to say on this subject as the years pass, but at this point would stress that Jack never drank alcohol in our house, except to join me in a glass of beer sometimes. We did not keep spirits, and this did not seem to distress him at all.

The morning after his first night with us we were surprised and amused to see that his bedroom mantelshelf was completely covered with rows of medicine bottles of all shapes and sizes. We never did discover when or how many of these multicoloured pills were consumed by Jack, or indeed for which indispositions.

We soon came to realize that he was the friendliest of companions, with a natural courteousness which never left him. Even our little dog Chippy, who usually bared his teeth at strangers, would lie for hours on Jack's lap with an expression of sheer bliss.

I don't think Jack was entirely at ease with children. He was not used to them, so it was not surprising that Judy and Nicholas were treated with a kindly aloofness at first. His natural shyness with the opposite sex ensured that this would be so towards Judy, then aged ten. He took a benevolent interest in Nicholas, especially when he grew older and went to school.

In these early days of our acquaintance the two children were rather in awe of Jack, following an incident at the telephone. He was talking to someone on a bad line as Judy and Nicholas were passing behind him, giggling and generally making a noise. Jack whipped round and shouted, 'Be QUIET!'. The culprits fled upstairs.

Jack had lived up to all my expectations: our long discussions on the works of other composers, the frequent sessions with the gramophone and at the piano, are memories I shall never forget. He did not treat me as an inferior in musical matters, which I was, but would even seek my opinion at times, as I will show later. Jack was an erudite musician — I was merely an enthusiastic amateur and indifferent pianist, yet he treated me as an equal.

And so we entered 1944, not knowing when the war would end, but certain that we had made a friend to be valued.

London was being blitzed in the New Year. I think that Jack was away in Kington for some months. My diary shows that I phoned him there on January 30th and he came down on February 22nd to stay with us for four days. I met him at Marylebone Station, where we took the 6.20 pm. train. We settled down in the blacked-out compartment, Jack puffing away as usual at his pipe, when I suddenly exclaimed, 'Damn! I've left my pipe at the office!' Jack fished in his raincoat pocket and pulled out a charred stump, saying 'Have this'. Very taken aback, I filled the object with tobacco and pretended to smoke!

The day after his arrival I went to bed with influenza, which was unfortunate because Jack and I were to go to a concert in London. Had I gone with him the events I am about to describe would almost certainly not have occurred.

He went to town alone, having expressed much concern for me, which somewhat consoled one for the loss of an evening out with him.

We expected him to return at about 11.30 pm. The hours passed with no sign of Jack. We decided that he was going to stay the night in town — for all we knew, the line from Marylebone might have been bombed. So we put out the light and tried to go to sleep.

Some considerable time later we heard an indescribable sound coming from afar in the inky blackness outside. At first it sounded like the wailing of a Banshee, and then of someone in dire distress. We exclaimed together, 'It's Jack!'.

Obviously he was in trouble of some kind, and 'flu' or not I must go and look for him. So, donning an overcoat and grabbing a torch, I opened the front door and went down the garden path, calling, 'Jack, where are you?'

Presently I could hear muffled groans coming from the field between us and the railway. So I walked with difficulty along the rough path outside our property and entered the field. Immediately to my left was a thick brier hedge. Jack was lying in the middle of this. I shone the torch and saw in what an awful state the poor chap was. His mackintosh was caught in the prickles and his face and hands were scratched and bloody. Without any words I heaved him up and away from the hedge, and putting his arm around my neck we stumbled towards the house. On the way his only muttered remark was, 'Where the hell have you been?' — to which I could think of no suitable reply!

I somehow got him into the house, put him in a chair, made up the fire, and went into the kitchen to make some strong black coffee. No sound came from Jack, and when I took the drink to him he was slumped in his chair. However, he drank the strong liquid and I was eventually able to coax him up the stairs to his bedroom, where I thankfully shut the door. As I walked along the passage to our bedroom there was a terrific thump as Jack collapsed on his bed.

There was little sleep for us that night, or what was left of it. Strange to say, I suffered no ill effect from my nocturnal wanderings in the chill night air and was able to appear at an early breakfast table, waiting for Jack to appear — apprehensive as to whether he would put in an appearance. But we need not have worried, for he burst in upon us as bright and cheerful as we were subdued. It was as if nothing untoward had happened the night before. We could only sit in dumbfounded silence while he talked.

Pushing back his chair and looking at his watch, which he always did with a pronounced lift of the elbow, he said brightly, 'I must catch the 8.10 to Marylebone as I've several urgent things to do in town to-day,' and abruptly left the room to get ready. After a cheery goodbye and a slam of the front door, he was gone. It seemed incredible. A few hours before, he had been helpless, dazed and almost rigid; and there he was now, trotting up to the station with a full day's events ahead of him!

It was not until a few years later that we heard the story of what had happened on that memorable night. Wherever Jack had been during the day, he eventually ended up at the 'M.M.' Club in the West End, which was run 'Mainly for Musicians' by Miss May Mukle, herself a cellist and former fellow student with my mother at the Royal Academy of Music.

Apparently Jack had stayed very late that evening until every other guest had left. He was in an alcoholic stupor by then, and Miss Mukle had the greatest difficulty in getting him upstairs to the street. She kept asking him where he was staying the night, but all Jack could mumble was 'Marylebone.' So she took the only course available and called a taxi, bundled him into it and told the driver which station to make for.

What has always puzzled me is how Jack was able to pay the driver, find his way to the correct train, and alight at Seer Green Halt in the blackout – let alone find our house, or nearly so!

Jack never once alluded to this sequence of events, and no embarrassment ensued from the incident.

During this period of the war we had an evacuee living with us, a young spinster who was secretary to a neighbour. She was a pleasant, if somewhat nervous, person. I am afraid she began to think we must be rather odd to be friendly with such a queer character as Jack Moeran. Not being musical herself, she did not have our sympathetic understanding of a creative mind, but I must admit that her suspicions were not entirely unfounded; as for instance when Jack appeared to have every intention of forcibly entering her bathroom, which was on the ground floor, while she was, until then, enjoying a hot bath.

All the doors in our house were of old cottage type and fitted with hand-made latches, not the usual knobs. These solid latches were noisy if not used gently. On this occasion of the abortive bathroom entry, we were all sitting in the drawing room listening to records when suddenly Jack leapt to his feet, dashed out of the room and across the hall to the bathroom-cum-lavatory door, where he rattled the latch violently to no avail. Scarcely believing his failure to obtain entry to what was, after all, a normal place of admittance, he backed several paces, and I was just in time to see him charge and almost wrench the offending latch off the door. We then heard a piteous cry from within the fortress, 'There's someone in here!' Without a word Jack returned and we continued our record session as if nothing had happened.

To the evacuee, who lived in a room upstairs and did not mix with the family, the trial by strength at her bathroom door must have made a lasting impression.

* * * * *

We heard nothing from Jack between February 26th and May 1st, when a postcard arrived dated April 30th:

> Oileam Ruash,
> Rockstown,
> Co. Cork
> I am staying on an island at the mouth of the Lee. The Spring here is glorious, day after day of hot sunshine. I have had bronchitis since I was over here, but now am so far recovered that I have been swimming in the sea (in April!).
> Jack

So that was where he had been all this time — in his beloved Kerry, from which only lack of funds or the expiration of his permit would force him to return.

Another postcard, dated May 22nd, confirmed this opinion:

> Kenmare,
> Kerry
> Thanks for your letter. I would love to have come with you to the Albert Hall, but I so far have failed to get a Permit to go over to England. I hope it may materialize in two or three weeks' time. Meanwhile, my isolation here is enforced.
> Jack

I had written him with an invitation to come to a Delius concert, but it was not to be.

Another postcard arrived within a fortnight. Evidently his exit from the monastery was delayed:

> Mount Melleray Abbey
> 4/6/44
> I have been here staying in this famous monastery (Trappist) since the middle of the week. There is Gregorian music being sung at various hours of the day and night. I return to-morrow to Kenmare.
> J.

A month later I received another postcard, dated July 11th:

Kington

I am back from Eire since last week: your letter of June 20th, has arrived here today, having been across and back from Ireland.

Thank you for what you are doing about the possibility of recording.

The Violin Concerto is being broadcast on the African wavelength at 8.30pm. on Friday. You should get it on the short wave.

I am going to Bedford for rehearsals on Thursday. I have just completed a set of five songs to poems of Seumas O'Sullivan.

Best wishes to you, Betty and family,
Jack

His expression of thanks referred to a plea I was making in *The Gramophone* for a recording of the Violin Concerto. We were not able to hear the short-wave broadcast. Jack's reference to the O'Sullivan song-cycle is interesting, and I will allude to this later when he brought the manuscript to our house. My diary records that on the same day that he wrote the above post-card he also phoned us from Kington — a spontaneous act very typical of him.

I must at this point have written to him, telling of my efforts to persuade Sammons to take up the Concerto, because we got another letter, dated August 26th:

Kington

Many thanks for your letter and kind offices on my behalf with your Pa-in-law. I shall certainly write to him very soon and I shall have to go and see him in London later when the R.C.M. begins. I am busy finishing off my *Sinfonietta*; nearly done now. I am not yet married. Peers won't be home for another month or so. She is still in the Middle East.

Yours,
Jack

They were not to be married for another eleven months. On September 23rd I received a letter of unusual interest:

Kington

Dear Lionel,

I feel rather guilty not having written to you for so long, but I have been, and still am, immersed in a spell of work at super pressure.

The result is that I have practically finished my small Symphony or Sinfonietta in three movements. Two more days copying out the fair copy of the last few pages of the Finale and it is done.

This means three works this year, a bumper year for me — the *Overture for a Masque*, the O'Sullivan song-cycle of seven songs, and now the *Sinfonietta*. I haven't heard the Overture yet: it was played several times by the Liverpool Philharmonic on tour when I was in Eire. I am daily expecting to get word of further opportunity of hearing it.

I wrote to Albert Sammons, but having mislaid your letter, I had to address him c/o R.C.M., so as I suppose they are still on vacation I don't know whether he got it yet.

I expect Peers home any time now. Her tour was due to finish at Cairo on Sept. 16th and she said she hoped to get a berth on the next home-going convoy after that.

I listened in to the new records of the Delius Concerto; I think they are splendid, and as a result I find I like the Concerto much more than I did before. Did you hear Iris Loveridge play my *Rhapsody* with the B.B.C. Northern Orchestra two weeks ago? She has made a new work of it, and it sounds quite different to that poor performance at Albert Hall last year.

> Best wishes to all,
> Jack

Musically speaking, this letter was the most interesting for a long while. Jack seldom discussed his own music with me, or anyone else, so any news of such importance was pure gold. It was a complete surprise to learn that he had been writing these works during our eighteen-month friendship; this reticence was so typical of him.

Jack's enthusiastic comments on Sammons' records of the Delius bring to mind his reservations in an early letter, and foreshadow many he would later retract.

On October 13th he came to stay for three nights, during which occurred an event of much interest — with comic overtones. He arrived later than we expected, in fact we had to keep postponing the evening meal. When he did arrive, it was obvious that he was in one of those dreamy moods induced by a lengthy visit to the bar at Marylebone Station. As he and I walked towards the piano, and Betty and Judy began to lay the supper, Jack paused at the sofa and leant over to pat our dog Mickey, murmuring words of endearment. This unexpected waft of alcoholic vapour was too much for Mickey, whose eyes took on a glazed look as he withdrew as far as the cushions would allow. It was amusing to see how the dog knew that Jack was somehow different that night.

Jack then sat down at the piano and said, 'I've brought along some songs I've just finished,' and propping up the inked-in manuscript on the music stand he opened the first page.

This unexpected treat was most exciting, and as his fingers moved over the introductory arpeggic in the piano part I wondered what would happen when the voice entered.

The result was beyond description. To the words, 'I will go out and meet the evening hours' he produced a wailing, tuneless drone that went on and on, continuing thus right through the seven songs. I will never hear its like again. Betty and Judy, especially the latter, were convulsed with suppressed laughter.

Despite this weird first performance of *Seven Poems of Seumas O'Sullivan*, I could see that they were very beautiful. They were published as a set of six songs in 1946, which means that we alone heard the omitted song on that memorable evening.

* * * * *

An unusually long gap now occurred, ending with a postcard dated December 5th:

> Thanks for your card. I was at the rehearsal of the Overture but not the performance, as I was conducting *Songs of Springtime* the same evening in Huddersfield. However, I listened in, and thought it went well. Groves is a very capable conductor.
>
> E.J.M.

I was not aware that Jack was a conductor, especially of such a top-notch choir. However, his next letter throws more light on this subject:

> Kington,
> Dec. 16./44
> Dear Betty and Lionel,
> Thank you very much for that lovely book. Sean O'Faolain is by far the best writer today in Ireland. I wonder if you ever read his novel about Cork City, *Bird Alone*?
> I was in London last week-end, but so full up that it would have been impossible to slip out to Seer Green. Literally, every moment was taken up. I had previously been up North before going to Norfolk for a four-day holiday among old friends. As you know, I used to live there at one time.
> I blossomed out as a conductor up in Yorkshire and conducted my *Songs of Springtime* in Huddersfield Town Hall. I think I gave satisfaction as I have been asked to go again on a future occasion and direct *Phyllida and Corydon*.

My word, what a wonderful choir, delightful to work with and miles easier than conducting an orchestra. I didn't even use a baton! The Liverpool Philharmonic are doing my Concerto twice, January 13th and a repeat on January 21st with Max Rostal. Barbirolli is mad keen to do it with Albert in the Spring and he told me he was going to do his damndest to goad the latter to agree to learn it. J.B. says he considers Albert is the one and only violinist for that work, but he is so anxious to perform it soon that I am terribly afraid that if Albert won't take it on he will go and do it with somebody else up North with the Hallé, although the B.B.C. have agreed not to do it until Albert has it ready.

The first performance of the *Sinfonietta* is fixed for the B.B.C. Symphony Concert on March 7th, with Barbirolli as guest conductor. Thank God we have escaped Boult for it!

A happy Christmas to you all,
Jack

He must have really enjoyed that conducting session, for otherwise it would have been an ordeal for such a shy character as Jack.

Sammons was never to play the Concerto with Barbirolli. The latter was evidently of my opinion that Albert was the artist to do it, but J B wouldn't have known, of course, that my father-in-law had already promised Betty and myself that he would take it on — it was only a matter of when.

It is interesting that Sir Adrian Boult subsequently recorded the *Sinfonietta*, in 1968; I am sure that Jack would have been pleased with this performance.

Having come to the end of another year's friendship with Jack, I will try once more to sift the wheat from the chaff. We had learnt that he was a very companionable man, whose company demanded one's whole attention. He had passed so many nights under our roof that he had come to be accepted as one of the family. Our two children had lost their earlier shyness with him, and he was at ease with them. We had almost worn out the gramophone, and few of my records remained unplayed. Indeed, I was constantly buying new ones of those composers I knew he liked, such as Roussel, Bloch, Bax, Butterworth, Sibelius, Debussy and Vaughan Williams. He adored the latter's *Pastoral Symphony*.

I had come to realize that the countryside, in all its moods, meant more to Jack than life itself — indeed he could not compose away from the rural scene; his favourite composers were similarly inspired.

His very personal brand of humour always delighted us, usually at mealtimes, and the frequent feats of mimicry would convulse the children.

With the one exception of that night when I had to rescue him from our hedge, Jack had shown little recourse to alcohol. He never drank spirits whilst with us, but on return from a day in town one could sense that total abstention had not been observed. This fact did not in any way spoil our evenings together – quite the reverse, for his mood would be one of mellow satisfaction.

I met Jack in town occasionally, sometimes at a convenient pub where he knew we would meet musician friends of his. I began to see that not all of these 'friends' were a good influence, and were not by any means confined to the musical profession. This one weakness in Jack's make-up, which was only apparent in certain circumstances, did nothing to impair his relations with my family at home – and he spent a lot of time with us over the years.

As I have said, Jack seldom talked about his own music, but I often used to wonder what composition was taking shape in his mind. I never saw any manuscript paper lying about, nor did he extemporize at our piano. He must have been able to 'hear' music clearly because he once told me that he wrote his sonata for two violins whilst lying in bed after an illness. Bearing in mind that he composed slowly, and that before long several major works were to appear, I think his mind must have been very active during this period. One has only to think of the forthcoming Cello Concerto, Cello Sonata and the *Serenade* to realize the truth of this supposition.

The year ahead – 1945 – was to be a momentous period for Jack, and by inference for my family also. The first news of his whereabouts came early in the New Year.

> Kington,
> January 10th 1945
> Dear Lionel,
> I think you have the miniature score of music of Bax's *Tintagel*. If so, please send it at once to me to the Adelphi Hotel, Liverpool. The piece is to be played there on Sunday and I hope to be at the concert. I understand they are also doing the lovely *Garden of Fand* on Saturday in the same programme as my Violin Concerto.

38

The Concerto, by the way, is going to be repeated at the Liverpool Philharmonic on Sunday week (or fortnight, I'm not sure which). I do not think Max Rostal will be my ideal interpreter. He is a fine artist but too German in outlook and tradition for my liking in music like mine.

I wonder whether Barbirolli has had any luck, or better luck than the B.B.C., in inducing Albert Sammons to learn it. He told me he was going to do his best to urge him to perform it with him at a Spring Hallé concert. I have persuaded the B.B.C. not to engage any other artist to play it for the present anyhow. The trouble is about Rostal that he has taken a great liking for it and I am afraid he may want to play it elsewhere, and I can't prevent this happening if he gets engagements to do so.

I was up in London last week – Thursday to Sunday. I had an idea of ringing you up suggesting coming down to Seer Green for the day on Sunday, but it was so vilely cold that as soon as Peers went off, which she had to do to play at concerts in East Anglia, I decided to come straight home.

I hope you are not getting V.2's arriving your way. I hear that a terrible lot of them fell in Essex or on the eastern suburbs of London itself and seemed to be in places as far apart as Staines and Pinner. They appear to be much more prevalent last week than my previous visit to London and, in fact, I was quite glad to leave.

All the best,
Jack

There is no doubt that Jack was very lucky to have his concerto regularly performed in war time, but his dogged determination to procure Sammons to play it clearly showed how he wanted the work to sound – that quality that only this artist brought to the Delius Violin Concerto, for instance.

It was interesting to learn that Peers had returned safely from the Middle East, and had stayed recently with Jack and his mother at Kington; but it was sad to realize that their time together on this occasion had been so brief.

Jack was imbued with natural good manners of a type rarely met with these days, so we were not surprised when Betty received the following postcard:

Liverpool,
January 15th 1945
Many thanks for 'Tintagel' which arrived in time for the rehearsal and concert. It was very good of you to go specially to post it.
J.M.

The next letter will show why he must have hurried home to Kington almost immediately:

Kington,
January 16th

Dear Lionel,

Many thanks for your letter. It was very good of you and Betty to go out specially and send off 'Tintagel' so that it reached me in time for Sunday's performance. I was very glad to hear that your papa-in-law has agreed to John B's proposal. I came straight back from Liverpool and did not go on to Manchester on Sunday, the reason being that I felt a bad cold coming on and wanted to get home: I am glad I did so for I shall be down and out for a day or two and it is better to be here in home comfort. The Violin Concerto is being repeated at Liverpool next Sunday, but much as I should like to hear it again on that lovely orchestra (Reg. Kell's clarinet playing in the third movement is literally heavenly), Liverpool is too far, especially as I shall be going up for the Symphony on Saturday week (27th). Rostal is a very fine artist, but even so, Albert Sammons will, I feel sure, make it sound as no one else can.

Anyhow, my Symphony is on Saturday 27th and the following day at the Sunday concert; Albert is down as soloist in Elgar's Concerto, so I will write and tell him I will be there. He may like to take the opportunity of discussing things, unless he is going back to London the same night.

Now I may as well tell you confidentially that we may be in a difficult situation before long. The Liverpool Phil. are keen on recording my Concerto with Decca and naturally they having had Max Rostal up to do it with them I am afraid they may want to go ahead. However, I do not think there is any immediate danger (A) as they are hardly likely to do much in the way of recording sessions while the concert season is in full swing and moreover (B) Sargent will be safely out of the way in U.S.A. from the beginning of Feb. till March 15th or so.

The point is that I was told in strict confidence by the secretary of the Society that they are on the point of signing up for recording with Decca and making a whole series of records. So just at the moment I dare not tell anybody, Walter Legge especially, as I was bound to secrecy.

But if and when the time comes and they want to record my Concerto with Rostal, I don't know how on earth I am going to prevent it unless it is possible to get H.M.V. to put it in hand by engaging Albert and Barbirolli first, thus forestalling the other proposal. But the awkward thing is that I was told by Fell (the Liverpool secretary) that they don't want it to get to Legge's ears that they are going to do recordings for the rival firm, so I can't open my mouth in that direction.

Well, I shall see Albert Sammons next Sunday week I hope and the following day Barbirolli in Manchester. By that time I hope it may not be necessary to keep this business secret. In some ways I wish Fell hadn't confided in me. I would have told him of my wish and hope that Albert S. would someday record my Concerto, only the awkward thing was that Max Rostal was in the room, the only other person present during the conversation! So you can judge what a quandary I was in when the proposal was made that my Concerto might be one of the works they make records of: it was Rostal who proposed it and Fell 'fell' for it. Rostal, you see, has already recorded for Decca. However, that is no reason why I believe Sammons shouldn't play for Decca, as I have an idea he has already done so.

Now you must be very discreet about this. When I said that the Liverpool are on the point of fixing up a contract with Decca I didn't mean necessarily for my Concerto immediately: I imagine they will want to make a splash with some purely orchestral items with Sargent and the orchestra alone, but it will be necessary to be forewarned.

You have been wonderfully good about putting forward a plea in 'The Gramophone' and elsewhere for the recording of my Concerto, but I would suggest that, for the moment you drop it, at any rate until pa-in-law has played it with John B., otherwise seeing that Rostal and Liverpool have just been doing it Decca's might jump at it and say 'Ha, let's record it quick while they have it in rehearsal and the repertoire and save all the trouble and expense of the orchestra having to re-learn it and a lot more rehearsals'.

I think you should burn this letter, and if Albert Sammons should be with you, use your discretion about anything you might say in the matter. Perhaps you had better say nothing at all to him just now as I shall be seeing him in ten days' time.

I wish though that he could have taken it on earlier and then if he had already played it and broadcast it, as the B.B.C. wanted him to, we should have had a fait accompli. I should have had my answer ready, i.e. 'I prefer Albert Sammons' rendering to anybody else's.'

I foresaw that something like this was bound to happen sooner or later owing to the success of my Symphony recordings. If only your respected parent-in-law would not have wasted so much time over such stuff as Sir G Dyson's Concerto! (For God's sake don't repeat this to him, or if you do don't say I said it.) But he has recently been playing it all over the place, only this month (or next) at Norwich Philharmonic. Why! If it were Walton's or the Bloch or Bartok I could understand it and applaud it, especially the former. I would simply love to hear him do the Walton and I hope he will, but Dyson! — — — words fail me!!

By the way, you say you saw a rocket fall. Did you actually see it fall or explode? I saw one explode in the air one afternoon when I was standing on Hampstead Heath looking down over London, but I should have thought that they travelled too fast to be seen falling. They are horrible things and they quite put the wind up me in London last Thursday fortnight when one came over about every 3/4 hour all evening.

I am so glad you liked 'Fand'.* Now there is a work that ought to be recorded. I have written to Bliss; he is on The British Council.

      Yours,
        Jack.

P.S. I think 'British Composers of our Time' is a mistake; much better to put an important British work more regularly and often into the symphony concert programmes. I don't believe in segregation.

They had British nights at the Proms at one period and I think they did a lot of harm to British music.

I don't know whether the B.B.C. mean to give me an innings in 'British Music of our Time', but I understand that there is to be a programme devoted to me in April or thereabouts at which Paddy Hadley is to spout or 'compère' as I think they call it now. I am glad you have the 'Hebrides'. I think it is a masterpiece among concert overtures, a really lovely imaginative work.

It is impossible, after a lapse of so many years, to check the truth of Jack's fears and forebodings over the fate of his Concerto in the hands of the two main recording companies. To the present generation this letter of Jack's might well be amusing, but when he wrote it he was a desperate man — one who could see all his dreams of the perfect interpretation of his beloved Concerto turning to ashes. With hindsight we can see that fate decided that Sammons never recorded this beautiful work. It should have stood, with the Elgar and Delius Concertos, among Sammons' finest and most personal recordings.

Meanwhile, Albert came to stay with us for a few days, on which occasion there came Geoffrey Tankard, a gifted amateur pianist who sometimes joined Albert in sonata recitals.

To my joy they began playing Jack's Concerto, and it soon became obvious why the latter was so keen to have this fine player as *the* interpreter of the work. There was a sweep of phrase and sweetness of tone so vital to a rhapsodic work of this nature, of which only this artist knew the instinctive secret.

The next letter explains a few weeks' silence:

---

* *The Garden of Fand*, the tone-poem by Sir Arnold Bax.

Kington,
Feb. 10th 1945

My dear Lionel,

I should have written earlier, but expected I should be seeing you in London as I had intended going up last week for a few days. In fact, I actually started, stayed the night with my brother at Leominster so as to catch the early train, but was stricken down with awful pains and had to stay two days in bed at his house. The doctor said I had picked up an epidemic germ which is going about.

I was to have spent last Sunday evening with your pa-in-law on the Concerto. Things are really materializing: we had a go at the score together last week at Liverpool. He gave a superb performance of the Elgar, but Sargent's accompanying with the orchestra was rather second-rate; he accompanied mine rather better the previous week! Anyhow, Sammons is now playing at the top of his form. I wonder if it would be convenient to Betty and yourself if I run down to Seer Green then for a night. I haven't seen you for ages. I long, too, to hear your new records. Peers won't be in Town that week so I shall be free to go out of Town. Naturally when she is at home I would not like to hurt her feelings by not spending as much time as possible with her.

Anyhow, she is going on tour to North-West Wales and I shall join her there at Harlech for next week-end. I need a change and a breath of fresh air will not come amiss.

Appalachia was done recently at Liverpool at a special concert with Beecham. They never told me or I would have gone. However, there are going to be some Beecham concerts there in June, probably with *A Song of the High Hills*. I shall not fail to be there! I am very well in with Liverpool these days; they have just asked me for a new work: so have their rivals, the Hallé!

Yours ever,
Jack

It was exhilarating to learn that our dream was materializing at last, and in no uncertain manner.

On February 14th and 15th he phoned me to discuss a possible visit to us, and his coming stay with Peers in Harlech.

To our surprise Jack failed to turn up! The following postcard explained the reason:

Harlech,
February 18th 1945

I am afraid I must postpone the pleasure of coming to see you as I shan't be coming Londonwards, but returning direct home on Tuesday. It is a very comfortable hotel here, but awful weather.

E.J.M.

On March 7th the *Sinfonietta* was broadcast — the first performance — by Barbirolli and the BBCSO*. The piano *Rhapsody* was also
broadcast on March 20th with Iris Loveridge, but in between these dates
came another letter:

> Kington,
> March 12th
>
> My dear Lionel,
>
> I must tell you that last week I spent a lovely evening with Albert Sammons.
> He already plays my Concerto marvellously. He played it through beautifully
> at his first attempt with me at the piano, after which he took Peers and myself
> out to dinner.
>
> Anyhow, when the time comes for him to perform it with orchestra, we
> shall hear such a rendering as it has never yet had.
>
> Iris Loveridge is going to do my Rhapsody next Tuesday at 7 pm. or
> thereabouts from Manchester again, so I hope you will get back from Town
> in time to hear it. I came across this little book in a shop in Shrewsbury the
> other day and at once thought of the boy at Seer Green! So please give it to him.
>
> The only new records I have acquired lately are Elgar's Cello Concerto.
> It is a wonderful study in orchestration of a very tricky kind i.e. how to
> accompany the cello on the orchestra without submerging it; that is what I
> got it for, but the playing of Beatrice Harrison in the solo part is not my ideal.
>
> I have ordered another Delius volume — that containing *Paris*. I hope it
> will come without breakages.
>
> Yours,
> Jack

What marvellous reading this made! Obviously Albert was really
getting to know the concerto in company with its composer.

The 'little book' Jack had sent for our son Nicholas was about trains,
and we thought it was a very thoughtful gesture.

Jack's remarks about the Elgar Cello Concerto remind me that he
also told me that he had studied the Dvorak Concerto with reference
to the orchestral scoring (he loved this composer's music anyway), and
the forthcoming Cello Concerto would show that he had benefited from
a close look at these masterpieces, for Jack's scoring is exemplary.

He was still using Kington as a base, for when a fortnight had passed
I received another letter:

---

* From the BBC studios at Bedford.

44

Kington,
26/3/45

Dear Lionel,

Many thanks for your letter, also thanks to Nicholas for his letter and drawing.

It is very kind of you to suggest my bringing Peers along some week-end. I am sure she will love it. When, I don't quite know, as from April 7th onwards she will be doing various engagements in this part of the country. However, we will fix it up for some time a little later in the Spring.

I saw Barbirolli last week and he tells me he is not only going to do the Concerto with Albert Sammons in Manchester but to go around with him playing it in other places. This, however, won't be this side of the Autumn.

I have just got some more records − Delius Society volume including *Paris*, and the Elgar Violin Concerto with Menuhin. Also, second-hand but in perfect condition, excerpts from Verdi's *Falstaff* and Bellini's *Norma*.

I saw Heddle Nash last week and he tells me he just recorded a few days ago two of my songs for H. M. V. Barbirolli promised to try and press Walter Legge about the Violin Concerto with himself and Sammons, so I hope we may be able to nip in the bud any Decca suggestions as to its recording from other quarters.

What I do want to get is some decent Beethoven Quartet recordings but they all seem to be by the Busch Quartet, whose playing I don't like. There are Lener recordings but I am told they are rather old and not such good method of recording as now-a-days.

Best wishes to you all,
Jack

I regret to say that Sammons did not play the Concerto with Barbirolli in Manchester, or anywhere else. It was to be Sir Adrian Boult who would conduct the two forthcoming performances.

In retrospect, it seems a pity that the Hallé was not allowed to play this work, because Jack had always had a close relationship with this orchestra, many of whose players he numbered among his friends, including the late Sir Hamilton Harty, and latterly John Barbirolli, who himself had tried so hard to play it with Britain's finest violinist.

Albert certainly intended to give further performances of the work, but the onset of Parkinson's disease brought his career to an end shortly after his two appearances with Boult.

Jack's record purchases were interesting − the Delius being a result of listening so often to my collection. The two Heddle Nash songs were *Diaphenia* and *The Sweet of the Year*, and were issued quite soon on a ten-inch HMV record, beautifully sung, and accompanied by Gerald Moore.

Peace was declared on May 7th followed by two days' public holiday. On May 28th I wrote to Jack, mainly about a projected holiday to be spent with him at Kington. We had discussed the subject on his last visit and he was very keen for us to go.

His reply was immediate: —

> Kington,
>> June 1st
>
> My dear Lionel,
>
> Thanks for your letter. It would be lovely if you and Betty were to come to these parts. The only accommodation left is a double room from 18th–26th of June at the Oxford Arms, a very comfortable small hotel three minutes' walk away from our house. I wish we could put you up, but just at that time and, in fact, in July also, it is impossible, as my mother has her hands full otherwise with relatives coming. You could not beat Kington for country walks and it is very handy for the Welsh Border, which begins just outside the little town. I shall be here June 18th to 26th but shan't be here at all after July, and you say July is not convenient to you, so I do hope you will see fit to take your holiday in June. I am ashamed to say that when I got your letter on Tuesday I was just catching a train to go away for a night and put it in my pocket unread and only discovered it today; but I have acted at once and went straight out to the Oxford Arms. They are absolutely booked up otherwise and as they want to know soon I am ringing you up to-night.
>
>> Yours ever,
>> Jack

He phoned us the next day and we said we would love to come on June 18th.

We did not communicate for the next fortnight, but as the days passed we became more and more excited. The prospect of being with Jack in that part of the country he loved so well, and had described in such glowing terms, increased our impatience to join him.

* * * * *

Our journey to Kington turned out to be without incident, there being one change at Leominster, for Kington lay on a branch line. I remember that the porter was delightfully vague about the time of the next train, and that we found his accent difficult to understand.

The second train took us through increasingly lovely scenery, and as we approached Radnorshire we saw the dark line of hills forming Radnor Forest, beyond which lay Wales.

Kington was a small station in those days and reminded us of our own Seer Green Halt. It served a charming little market town situated in the Welsh Marches, the neutral ground between the Welsh and English and within two miles of the Border. It lies in a valley some 510 feet above sea level and is sheltered on the north and west by Bradnor Hill and Hergest Ridge, hills which rise to 1300 and 1400 feet respectively. The wonderful views from these hills embrace the Brecon Beacons, the Black Mountains, and the Malvern Hills. We were to see this vast panorama during our visit.

The town consisted of one long street extending from St Mary's Church to the railway station, and on that sunny afternoon in 1945 Betty and I carried our bags along the main street at about 5.30pm. looking for the Oxford Arms Hotel, which we found without difficulty, and booked ourselves in. After supper we went for a long exploratory walk.

The next morning, after breakfast, Jack came breezing into the hotel, dressed in comfortable tweeds and looking remarkably fit. After enquiring about our journey and the state of our accommodation, he asked us to tea at his family's house.

The Moeran property was approached by an inclined drive at the head of which stood 'Gravel Hill', a solid, well-proportioned Georgian residence, and the grounds appeared to be extensive.

Jack led us into the drawing room, where we were introduced to his mother. She was a small, white-haired old lady, not very like Jack in features I seem to remember. After tea we strolled round the well-kept gardens and noticed a smooth croquet lawn. Jack saw our interest in the latter and suggested a game, proceeding indoors to fetch the mallets and balls.

After a while he emerged clad in a wide-brimmed straw hat, looking very much like a retired Army officer from the North West Frontier.

We thoroughly enjoyed those games of croquet. The whole atmosphere of the house and gardens conveyed a sense of tranquillity, and it was hard to realize that the greatest war in history was only just over.

The next day we took some more walks, and after lunch Jack appeared and said that he was very anxious for us to meet Dr Jobson, his doctor and friend, and that the latter would call for us at the hotel shortly.

Jack had often talked about Dick Jobson, of whom he was obviously very fond. I was to learn that Dick knew a lot more about Jack's troubles than we did.

When Jack exclaimed 'Here comes Dick!' we saw a young figure striding along the High Street waving cheerily, and we moved forward to meet him. After introductions we soon became impressed by this family doctor, who radiated friendly goodwill.

Dick Jobson took us all in his car to New Radnor, where he lived with his parents, and from where he practised. The house we came to was different in every respect from the Moerans'. It was situated at the foot of what appeared to us was a small mountain, which brooded over the house like a frown. I wondered whether avalanches of snow ever threatened the inmates of this isolated dwelling.

Jack could not have brought us to a nicer family. It is rare to meet people who, from the first moment, seem to form a rapport with their new guests. We found Dick's parents to be most likeable, and Mrs Jobson seemed attracted to Betty and gave her a lot of attention. I soon found that Dick's hobbies coincided with mine, for he loved music, model trains and photography. He also played the clarinet, a feat I couldn't emulate.

I remember that he had built a beautiful brass model traction engine which really worked by steam, and was capable of pulling a truck with someone sitting aboard. Unfortunately the engine was under repair that day so we were not able to have a ride.

Like myself, he had been smitten by Jack's music, and when he came to be consulted by the composer a firm friendship ensued.

The next day there occurred an event of considerable interest. Jack took us along a passage to his study, the door of which was covered both sides with green baize for sound insulation. The room itself was rather small, and the sun flooded through the windows overlooking the garden. The first thing I noticed was an upright Bechstein piano opposite the door. There was a table in the centre of the room on which lay sheets of music manuscript and an oak silver-mounted bookend (which would become mine after Jack's death). Several pipes and a tobacco jar stood on the table. Music scores seemed to be everywhere, yet there was no impression of untidiness.

My thoughts were interrupted by Jack saying, 'Would you mind timing a piece of mine? It's for the information of the publishers'. I said, 'Rather, I'd love to'. He picked up a sheaf of manuscript from the top of a music cabinet and propped them up on the piano's music stand. The score was still in pencil.

He turned back the top edges of the pages for ease of quick turn-over and said quietly, 'This is my new Cello Concerto that I've written for Peers. Novello's are worrying the life out of me to get this to them because the first performance is already booked'.

'Ye Gods', I thought, 'I'm probably the first person to have heard this piece right through!' Afterwards I realized that Peers must have gone through the work with Jack at some time or other. Still, to be one of two people who first shared this Concerto with Jack was, with one later exception, the musical highlight of our friendship.

I placed my watch on the edge of the keyboard and Jack started to play, humming the cello part as best he could. He preferred to turn the pages himself, so all I had to do was watch my timepiece and savour a precious experience.

As the work proceeded I could tell that he had excelled himself, and that the growing number of Moeran lovers would not be disappointed.

We had reached about the middle of the first movement when Jack, snatching at a page to turn over, pulled all the loose manuscript off the piano and on to the floor, where it lay in scattered confusion. 'Damn', shouted Jack, 'Now we've got to start all over again'. So we did, this time without any mishaps.

This work impressed me a lot. Before starting the slow movement he turned to me and said in the pontifical manner he sometimes used, 'Influenced by Beethoven'. At the time I found this remark somewhat puzzling and wondered what he meant, and as we continued through this lovely movement I could not hear any resemblance to the German master.

When the session came to an end and the duration in minutes had been noted by Jack, I was still at a loss to understand his remark.

It was not until a few years later that I found the answer to the puzzle — and then by sheer chance. I had bought the nine Beethoven Symphonies arranged for two hands at the piano; and when I came to the slow movement of the Ninth I suddenly saw what Jack had meant, for there, in the first bars, lay a chord pattern with which I was so familiar in the piano reduction of the Cello Concerto. Both works invoked a similar feeling, though no imitation was present, and after these few bars the music was pure 'Jack' in his best Irish idiom. Despite this discovery I often wonder why he bothered to claim such a tenuous influence; which I must stress can only be readily spotted from the piano. I would dearly have liked to discuss this with Jack, but by then he was dead.

On one day of our visit he walked with us to Kington Church, an interesting old building; but my chief memory is of the delight that Jack took in showing us around the graveyard and especially the inscriptions of the tombstones. He knew just where the oddest examples could be found and read them out with much relish.

Another enjoyable trip was when he took us out beyond Radnor by train, and thence by bus to a spot from which we climbed up and up, seemingly above the world, until the ground flattened out to give us superb views for miles around in all directions. I remember Jack pointing and saying, 'Over there is Elgar country, and there, Housman country.' Most interesting of all was when he said, 'The inspiration for my *Sinfonietta* came to me up here, especially the middle movement, which should be played at a brisk walking pace — as we are doing now.' Sometimes I hear performances of this work where this movement is taken too slowly.

Suddenly we spotted an awesome sight. We were standing on the highest plateau for miles around and from our vantage point, and to my horror there appeared a line of horses with tails swishing and long bushy manes flying behind, and coming towards us in a menacing circle. The thudding of their hoofs and the way they appeared to be biting each other's rear quarters with bared teeth was most alarming. There was no way of escape, no hedge or tree to hide behind, and Jack and I couldn't run anyway, — with our 'gammy' legs and walking sticks.

Jack seemed quite unmoved by this frightening spectacle and said calmly, 'Those are mountain ponies. They're left up here all summer to fend for themselves, and are only led down to the lower fields when winter comes.' Meanwhile the wretched animals were storming ever nearer, and when the position became desperate Jack was inspired to shout, 'Now's the time to take a snapshot!'. True, I did have my camera with me, but wild horses, let alone mountain ponies, would not have induced me to become a wild-life photographer just then!

50

Luckily for us the prancing, frothing beasts, still chasing each other in a circle, were receding to the edge of the plateau and disappeared over the edge.

'Thank God for that!' I said.

'Oh! they usually behave like that,' replied Jack. 'As a matter of fact, I heard that two people were killed up here last year. Those ponies are completely wild, and have to fend for themselves'.

That other hazards still lay around us we were not to discover until we had descended to the lower fields and made our exit through a barred gate, at the side of which was a notice-board fixed to a post. The notice read, 'Beware of unexploded mines'.

Large numbers of American troops had descended on this area during the late war, and the last of them had only just left before we arrived. In fact, their exit was so recent that much of their equipment − blankets, towels, cooking utensils, etc. − was being sold cheap at the local American hospital.

We arrived back at the hotel very tired, but with many happy memories.

I must mention also that before we took our seats in the little train that ran between Kington and New Radnor, Jack said, 'I must introduce you to the engine driver; he's an old friend of mine'. So we walked along the platform to the little open-cab tank engine, and Jack, with his very personal brand of courtesy, introduced us to the equally polite driver, something almost inconceivable today, even if this particular branch line does still exist.

The remainder of this visit to Kington was occupied with more gatherings at the Jobsons, with tea, walks and croquet with Jack. But all too soon we had to depart with the sad feeling that we would probably never come to these lovely parts again.

* * * * *

On the day following our return home I posted my score of Bax's Third Symphony to Jack, who had asked for its loan, and which brought the usual quick reply:

Kington,
July 3rd/45

Dear Lionel,

Many thanks for the Bax score.

As the mushroom season approaches I am presenting you with this little book which I got the other day in Llandrindod Wells. I also have another copy of my own.

Appalachia was glorious on Saturday in spite of the fact that on one occasion the chorus came in too soon.

Best wishes,
Jack

The 'little book' was devoted to the subject of edible fungi. This may seem strange, but Jack had expressed his enthusiasm for fungi on several occasions, and much enjoyed gathering mushrooms in the fields around our house, and pointing out which were poisonous.

At about this time Peers wrote to us to thank Betty and me for a set of cut-glass we had sent as a wedding present: —

55 Belsize Lane,
N.W.3
July 21st

Dear Mr. Hill, Betty, Judy and Nicholas,

Thank you so very much for your lovely and most acceptable wedding present.

I have written and told Jack about our wealth of glass. He has taken my mother to Kington in preparation for what he calls 'Der Tag', so I am left to lone confusion coping with workmen, big ends, and suchlike.

You must all come and christen the glasses when we return.

Yours with again many thanks,
Peers Coetmore

We were not to see him for a month. On July 26th, he and Peers were married.

Jack spent the previous night with Dick Jobson; Peers at the Vicarage with her mother and Jack's parent. In later years Dick related how Jack had told him that the marriage was a disaster, and that in reply to Dick's 'Why go on with it?' he had said 'I have given my word as a gentleman. I cannot break my word' — a characteristic remark of the kind his friends found so endearing.

The notice in *The Daily Telegraph* read: —

52

MOERAN – COETMORE. On July 26th 1945, at Kington Parish Church, Herefordshire; ERNEST JOHN, younger son of the late Rev. J. W. W. Moeran and Mrs. Moeran, to Kathleen Peers (Peers Coetmore), younger daughter of the late STANLEY COETMORE JONES and Mrs. Coetmore Jones.

After the ceremony they spent a motoring honeymoon in Wales, which Peers, the daughter of a Welsh father, was anxious to show Jack. They made the journey in a pre-war Wolseley Hornet, a veteran of unpredictable habits of which only Peers knew the secret. She had visited us several times in this old 'banger' and seemed very proud of it.

On July 29th, Betty received the following letter from Mrs Jobson:

New Radnor

Dear Mrs. Hill,

Dick played the Brahms Quintet for me a few evenings ago and my thoughts went at once to you. I shall always think of you when I hear it. It was very sweet of you to write and I appreciated your letter greatly. Life has so much that is beautiful to offer us; I realize it more and more as I grow older. A home that is a real home is one of the beautiful things, but I fear that these days many people have not the vision to see it. Modern Woman does not appreciate this privilege.

Jack Moeran was married on Thursday 26th. It was a very quiet affair. Dick was Best Man. Pat Ryan was unable to come along. It simply *poured* with rain all day long but the rain did not damp the party. The bride and groom went to Bala, where they found sunshine and fair weather.

I hope we may meet again in the not too distant future.

With very kind regards,
Sincerely yours,
Grace Jobson

On August 26th, Jack and Peers motored down to see us, both looking fit and happy. Once again the tomboy in Peers was in evidence as she chased our children all over the garden, to shrieks of excitement.

Jack beamed on everybody that day in the manner he often displayed when, in his opinion, all was right with the world.

Over lunch they gave us a graphic account of their journey through Wales, and of some amusing incidents that had occurred. One of these was the way the Wolseley Hornet, once stopped, would not re-start until someone had given her bonnet a sharp blow. Apparently this always did the trick!

I do not know if this was Jack's first visit to the glories of North Wales, but I do remember how impressed he was by the scenery.

It was a happy day. The war was over, they were just married, and in two days' time Albert was going to play Jack's Concerto at the Proms. All the anxiety and hard work of the past months were about to bear fruit. No wonder Jack was beaming, for had he not also completed his Cello Concerto, which he must have known in his heart would be a worthy companion to the Violin Concerto?

Yes, that day in our house in the country was probably the happiest that Jack and Peers ever spent, and I am glad of it.

On Tuesday, August 28th, came the great event; Sammons gave a superb rendering of the Concerto, and the audience were most enthusiastic. How thrilled Jack was can be seen from his letter to Albert a few days later:

> 55 Belsize Lane,
> 1/9/45
>
> My dear Albert,
> Now that what I had so long looked forward to, namely to hear my Concerto played by yourself, has in fact happened, please let me thank you from the bottom of my heart for your superb playing of it. The poetry which seems to be instinctive in your conception of it, and which I have always felt, I am now assured that you are the only one to play it. Apart from this, the trouble and labour you have put into the study of my Concerto.
>
> And now I look forward to hearing you do it with John Barbirolli and his Hallé players under rehearsal conditions which I suppose are unique in this country.
>
> > Yours with the utmost gratitude and admiration,
> > Jack

I would like to quote the notice which appeared in the *Daily Telegraph* by F. Bonavia-Hunt, a much respected music critic of this period:

ALBERT SAMMONS AS SOLOIST

An attraction at last night's Albert Hall concert was the Violin Concerto of E. J. Moeran, which was first heard at a concert of the Royal Philharmonic Society, when it was played by Arthur Catterall.

This time the soloist was Albert Sammons, whose style and temperament differ considerably from Mr. Catterall's, but who was equally successful in revealing the many fine aspects of this thoughtful work.

Mr. Sammons excelled especially in the tranquil mood of the last section — a conception of much beauty and originality which made an immediate appeal to the audience.

One is struck by the humble tone of Jack's letter to Albert — a sure sign of the true creative artist. It is also worth noting his use of the words 'poetry' and 'instinctive', which were the attributes I found so appealing when Moeran's music first made its impression on me.

Note also that the Hallé Orchestra and Barbirolli are never far away from Jack's thoughts. His attitude was that he knew these players individually and that, therefore, they understood his music. It was as simple as that. The recent performance under Sir Adrian Boult was adequate under poor rehearsal conditions, but only the Hallé would learn and play it with affection and thus be the perfect partners for his other ideal artist – Sammons.

What a tragedy it is that this never materialized. Jack's letter to Albert was the second to come from 55 Belsize Lane, NW3, which belonged to Peers, and was situated in a rather countrified position behind a high brick wall, the whole property being approached along a tree-lined narrow lane. One entered by means of a large door in the wall, and found oneself looking at a mews cottage. Most of the ground floor was taken up by a large airy studio, the remainder being the kitchen and usual offices. The sleeping quarters, of course, were upstairs, though I never saw these.

Over the next three years I was to visit this studio frequently, always in the daytime, and would hear Jack and Peers practising the Cello Concerto among other works. Some of his records had come from Kington to the studio, where there was a radiogram, and we often played these. I was glad to see two albums of Delius in evidence.

It is a treasured memory that on several occasions I was able to hear these two playing the Cello Concerto before the first public performance, thus forming a perfect sequel to my timing of the work at Kington earlier in that year.

The next letter from Jack also came from the studio:

> 55 Belsize Lane,
> October 31st 1945
>
> Dear Lionel,
> Many thanks for your letter and for the prints. In one I look the image of Albert Coates, both facially and in stance. Please let me have your office telephone number on a postcard. Then I will ring you up one morning and suggest lunch somewhere in Hampstead.
>   We shall be away at Southsea next week Mon. – Thurs. then back here until

our departure for Eire on Mon. fortnight, 19th Nov. The new Concerto is on Sunday afternoon the 25th from the Capitol Theatre, Dublin. If you have an aerial you can get it; at least, I got last Sunday's concert from the same source very well at Ledbury with an aerial, but it is impossible without.

    Best wishes to all,

    Jack

There were no more letters to come from Jack for the remainder of the year, but on November 14th I lunched with him and Peers at the studio, and on the 19th they left for Dublin, where she played the Concerto on the 25th. Dick Jobson told me that this premiere performance was well received. From this date until the beginning of February they remained in Eire, and during this period Jack promised Peers to write a cello sonata for her.

On the way to Eire, Jack found time to return another Bax score which I had lent him. This lay on our doormat, together with an almost illegible pencil note which he had written against our front door. He and Peers had evidently called whilst we were out. This meticulous care of other people's property was one of his endearing qualities.

* * * * *

And so this very significant year for Jack drew to a close. For us it perhaps marked the zenith of our seven years' friendship with him. A faint glimmer of the course events were to take can be seen in his next letter, in which he bemoans the lack of a suitable venue for composition.

If ever there was a composer who demanded sympathetic surroundings in which to call down inspiration, it was Jack. He often said it was impossible for him to compose in a town, and it was uncanny how subtly his music reflected the nature of his surroundings — from the early piano pieces to the late orchestral works, and give his music (the English and Irish idioms) the charm of sincere lyrical feeling. In the country he could breathe, and find the music which lay impatiently just below the surface.

A little later we were to try and find a suitable spot in the Chilterns where he could obtain peace and quiet, but nothing came of this. I often wonder whether this was the turning point in what was to be a gradual descent to complete stagnation.

56

On December 31st, Clarence Raybould and the BBC SO broadcast the Symphony in G Minor on the London, Scottish and Midland wavelengths.

The following day, January 1st, 1946, I rang Jack's mother at Kington in case he was there, hoping to discuss the previous day's broadcast with him, only to be told that he was still in Eire.

A further broadcast of Jack's music took place on January 15th, when Iris Loveridge played *Windmills* in a programme called 'Serenade'.

I am not sure exactly when he returned to England, but his next letter, the one I referred to above, is full of interest:

Ledbury
February 10th 1946

Dear Lionel,

Many thanks for your letter and enclosure. I saw Legge of H.M.V. the other day: he has not heard the *Sinfonietta* so I am afraid we shall not get much further in that quarter yet.

Sargent gave a magnificent performance of it two weeks ago to-day, as did Raybould at the People's Palace in November.

There are any amount of performances of it booked ahead in various places and it is a great pity the gramophone people don't do something to get to know what goes on.

I didn't hear my Symphony on December 31st as I was in Kenmare. Nobody bothered to let me know about it.

I started work on a new symphony there, but I see no prospect of going on with it, nor with any composition in the immediate future. I have nowhere to work. I can't do anything at all in London, and until I can find some pied-a-terre in peace and quiet I can't compose.

I had to withdraw the Cello Concerto from the Cambridge* for to-day as I stipulated for adequate rehearsal, and this was not forthcoming. Peers comes down here to-night and goes on a C.E.M.A. tour in Wales for two weeks starting to-morrow. I am staying here a few days more and then coming to London to attend to things, when I will ring you up.

Yours,
Jack

---

* The Cambridge Theatre

We already knew from Dick that Jack had started work on his Second Symphony, but as is clear from the letter he could not settle down in a congenial place in which to compose. Also very remarkable was the way he withdrew the performance of the Cello Concerto because of insufficient rehearsal − surely an act of high artistic self-denial.

Four days later I visited Webster & Girling, the record shop in Upper Baker Street to which I had taken Jack before, and was told I had just missed him. This was a pity, as we were not to meet again until early April.

The Symphony was broadcast again on February 2nd under the baton of Charles Groves.

Albert Sammons had been engaged to play the Violin Concerto up North in early March, but was prevented from doing so by a bout of 'flu.

I duly met Jack on April 4th, when we went together to see Vaughan Williams' opera *Sir John in Love* at Sadler's Wells. Roderick Jones sang Falstaff and the conductor was Lawrence Collingwood. I remember that Cecil Gray came to sit with us in the front stalls, and that every seat in the house seemed to be taken. I can still see Jack sitting on the edge of his seat during the interval between acts, when the lights were dimmed and the orchestra continued to play. As in Wagner, this inter-act music is an important part of the whole opera, but is rarely treated as such by many audiences in this country.

On this occasion the usual chattering had broken out around us, and Jack, who was leaning forward on his seat to catch every note from the orchestra, suddenly turned round and emitted a long, extremely loud and penetrating 'Sh-ss-sh!' The whole house became deathly quiet − I sat aghast! Quite unabashed, Jack resumed his absorption with the orchestra, and amazingly a discreet silence reigned for the rest of the Interlude.

This unusual behaviour of Jack's, normally the quietest of men, pleased me immensely. How many times in the past had one suffered in silence from philistine audiences − but Jack's instant remedy had a lot to recommend it.

The Cello Concerto was broadcast on April 10th from The People's Palace, Peers of course being the soloist. I was there to see the work go down well with the audience.

They both paid us a visit in the Wolesley Hornet on April 14th; there was much to talk about.

58

My father-in-law gave his second performance of the Violin Concerto on April 28th, this time from Norwich. Sir Adrian Boult conducted the BBC Symphony Orchestra and the concert was broadcast. This was too good an opportunity to miss, so I made hasty arrangements with a studio to record the concert for my private use. This was duly carried out, and is probably the only copy in existence with the exception of a tape transfer which I have placed with The British Institute of Recorded Sound, for permanent storage and future use by students and admirers.

I took Betty and my mother to hear Jack's *Sinfonietta* at Hammersmith on April 29th, where it was given a lively performance by Anthony Bernard. I was able to tell Jack about this and other recent events when I had lunch with him and Peers at Swiss Cottage on May 1st. It was then that he gave me a letter he had received from Sweden, which is worth quoting: —

(*extract*)

> Uppsala,
> Sweden
>
> Dear Sir,
> On behalf of Varmlands Musical Club, I should like to tell you how much we admire and like your music, and how much we esteem its composer.
>
> Since becoming familiar with the two recorded compositions we started something which I might about call a Moeran cult. We began to listen to musical broadcasts with even more zeal, and informed one another as quickly as possible when a work of yours was discovered either in the printed foreign programme or direct on the air. In this way we actually managed to hear a *Rhapsody* for piano and orchestra and a Violin Concerto; some of my friends have even been so fortunate as to hear some of your chamber music, including a string quartet. On December 31st we were lucky enough to hear a performance of your Symphony. It was a tremendous experience.
>
> When we write to you, we do it not only to thank you for what you have given us. We would also be very grateful to know which of your other works have been recorded, now that trade connections with England seem at last to have been resumed.
>
> There is a very great interest in records of your work over here — so great that the String Trio recorded by Columbia was actually smuggled into Sweden in the very thick of the war. A young English pilot who had been interned in Sweden for a time was persuaded to flout the regulations and take with him the longed-for records on his return flight from Great Britain to Dalecaria, where they now are.

Several sets of your Symphony arrived quite recently in Stockholm. It was not nearly enough; needless to say, they are already sold out.

Obviously Jack was very pleased with this evidence of interest from abroad.

Shortly after this chance meeting I wrote to him suggesting that perhaps I might write to Barbirolli about a possible recording for the Violin Concerto by himself and Sammons. Jack's reply was as follows:

> The New Inn,
> Rockland-St.-Mary
> Norfolk.
> June 11th 1946
>
> Dear Lionel,
> Many thanks for your letter. Do by all means write to Barbirolli if you think it will do any good. As for July 6th (Saturday) I think we can look you up on the way back from Cheltenham, provided the Wolsey Hornet continues to function by then.
>
> I am conducting my *Sinfonietta* there on the evening of the 5th. In any case Seer Green is almost en route travelling via Oxford and the Wycombes.
>
> Yours ever,
> Jack

I did write to Barbirolli, but before quoting his reply I must record that on July 6th we had the great pleasure of a visit by Jack and Peers, and Albert Sammons happened to be there as well. This wonderful event was memorable for the playing of my private records of the Violin Concerto. In my wildest dreams I had never dared to hope for such a meeting, and I can still remember how composer and violinist listened to the Concerto; their intense enjoyment was a source of great happiness to Betty and myself.

The reply from Barbirolli contained at least the knowledge that he was keen to record the Concerto:

> The Hallé Concerts Society,
> Manchester, 2.
> July 17th 1946
>
> Dear Mr. Hill,
> Thank you for your letter, with which I sympathise most sincerely and deeply.
> Nobody regrets more than I your father-in-law's firm decision and nobody would be happier than I if I could do anything to make him change his mind.

60

Alas, I have written to him trying to persuade him at least to open our Hallé season with me in October – without success. I have now written again to him to say that if he feels, after a rest, that he would record the Moeran with us, I would move Heaven and Earth to get this done by the Gramophone Society. I love the Moeran Concerto and I can very well imagine what Albert's performance of this work must be – wonderful I am sure. I assure you that any pushing I can do, I shall do; but the only hitch is that if Albert is really adament as alas he seems to be – that seems to be the end of it. I shall see what sort of reaction he has to my last letter.

I only hope something may come of our efforts!

Yours sincerely,

John Barbirolli

* * * * *

It was at about this time that I became the music critic for a new musical paper, and began the enjoyable occupation of covering various concerts around London, and writing articles on general musical subjects. For this purpose I used the pseudonym of 'Robin Lea'. To begin with, Jack knew nothing of this new activity of mine and a little incident that arose when he and Peers paid us a visit caused me much amusement. They breezed into the sitting room and Jack, waving a newspaper, exclaimed,

'Who is this chap writing in this new paper?' Taken completely by surprise, all I could reply was, 'What do you think of his stuff?'

'Not bad,' said Jack, 'He's got something to say at any rate.' Much relieved I glanced at Peers, who was watching intently my reddening face. With a woman's disconcerting intuition she said: 'It's you, isn't it?'

I had to confess, which caused Jack to exclaim, 'Well I'm damned!' and the incident closed in hearty laughter. I remember suggesting that I could perhaps publish the laudatory letter that Jack had received from fans in Sweden, but for some curious reason he was against this idea, which I still think was a mistake on his part.

During lunch we got onto the subject of Walton's music, and especially *Belshazzar's Feast*. After a moment of silence Jack looked up at me across the table and said with one of his sweetest smiles, 'Hardly the music of a eunuch?'

He had a great admiration for Walton, especially his Violin Concerto, and although Jack was usually attracted by the folk-song school of British composers, Walton was a notable exception.

I saw him fairly often in London during the next month or so, sometimes at Belsize Lane or in a pub in the West End. One occasion I remember clearly was when we met Brian Easdale, the composer, in a little restaurant at Swiss Cottage. It was he who would write the music for that excellent film *The Red Shoes*, starring Moira Shearer and with Sir Thomas Beecham conducting the score. Jack and I noticed that a miniature score of Richard Strauss was propped against Easdale's glass of water, and as we sat down he nodded at the score, saying 'I'm getting some ideas on orchestration.' I noticed Jack smiling to himself − if only one could describe that smile of his, which was never far away, and more expressive than words.

On September 29th the BBC opened its Third Programme. Jack and I were very excited by the prospect of a channel devoted to serious music.

In the autumn of this year the second Delius Festival took place (the first had occurred in 1929, when I was able to attend every concert). I was able to go to the present series as the critic for my paper. Jack also came to some of the concerts, either at the Albert Hall or the Central Hall, Westminster.

On November 4th I went to the second Delius concert with Albert Sammons and his wife, and they managed to gain access to Beecham in his heavily-guarded Artist's Room during the interval, and I was introduced to the great man. I met Jack after the concert and told him about this and he said 'You lucky beggar!'

He asked me to call at the Belsize Lane studio the next day in order to adjust the pick-up of his radiogram. I always enjoyed these visits because music was usually discussed or played. Peers was not always present for she had many engagements at this period, so Jack and I used to go out for our meals. At other times I would have lunch with both of them at the studio, and I recall that on one occasion we were discussing the music of Bax. I said that his thick textures worried me at times and turning to Peers I remarked, 'I think Jack is worth two of Bax!' Peers replied instantly, 'Oh, so do I.' I know that this was a wild statement on my part, but at the time I meant it, and glanced in Jack's direction. He didn't utter a word, but had gone a profuse pink − and I was never fonder of him than at that moment.

One day at about this time he gave me a copy of a periodical in which was an article by him about collecting folk-songs in East Anglia. It is too long to quote in full, but as it contains much that is helpful to an understanding, both of his early musical influences and his character, I will give the following extract:

In the years immediately preceding the first world war, there took place in London some remarkable choral and orchestral concerts at which the programmes consisted largely of British music. Many first performances of the works of such composers as Holst, Vaughan Williams, Arnold Bax and Percy Grainger, names at that time quite unfamiliar to the general public, were given at this time.

Having just left school, I had come to London as a student at the Royal College of Music; apart from a certain amount of Stanford and Elgar, I knew nothing of the renaissance that had been taking place in music in this country. So one winter's evening, when I had been to St. Paul's Cathedral intending to hear Bach's Passion music and failed to obtain a seat there, feeling in the mood for any music rather than none at all, I went to the Queen's Hall, where there was a Balfour Gardiner concert, prepared to be bored stiff. But, on the contrary, I was so filled with enthusiasm, and so much moved by some of the music I heard that night, that from then on I made a point of missing no more of these concerts.

Among other works I heard was a Rhapsody of Vaughan Williams, based on songs recently collected in Norfolk by this composer. It was my first experience of a serious orchestral composition actually based on English folk-song, and it caused a profound effect on my outlook as a young student of musical composition. This, and other works which I encountered at these concerts, though not all based on actual folk music, seemed to me to express the very spirit of the English countryside as I then knew it. My home at this time was in Norfolk, where my father was vicar of a country parish, so I determined to lose no time in rescuing from oblivion any further folk songs that remained undiscovered.

I soon found that in the part of the country where I was living at the time, there was not much spontaneous singing of the old songs still going on. In any case, the 1914 war intervened to put a stop to my activities for the time being. As most of what I heard had been sung to be by elderly men, who assured me old songs were fast dying out, by the time the war was over I assumed there was no more to be had, and did not immediately make any serious efforts at collecting folk-songs.

However, when I was visiting East Norfolk in the autumn of 1921 I received from a folk-song enthusiast, not himself a musician with the necessary knack of committing tunes to paper, an S.O.S. for me to come at once to Stalham.

It turned out that accidentally he had overheard an old roadmender singing softly to himself as he was breaking stones. Thus I met the late Bob Miller, known for miles around the country as 'Jolt'. Bob admitted that he knew a few 'Old 'uns', but he insisted that he had not really been singing, but just 'A-tuning over to himself'. However, he was only too willing to sing to me under proper conditions and suggested my spending the evening with him in the Catfield 'White Hart' or the 'Windmill' at Sutton.

Old Jolt dearly loved conviviality, and was always at his best in company; he knew it, and liked an audience. In fact, he was incapable of remembering anything at all 'à deux'. He required the atmosphere of a room full of kindred souls who would listen with appreciation, and he expected his full share of applause. At the same time he was a keen listener when somebody else held the floor in song or story. Anything in the way of interruption and he would wither the offender with the glance of an autocrat. He gave me many very interesting songs, some of which were hitherto unpublished.

Bob Miller was an old bachelor of absolute integrity, but it delighted him, especially late in the evening, to take on the semblance of a disreputable character, and it was invariably just about closing time when he would come out with something to suit his rakish humour.

This singer, by his enthusiasm and personality, opened the way to a series of convivial evenings at which I soon found out that the art of folk singing, in this corner of Norfolk at any rate, was still flourishing in the 1920s.

About the third occasion on which I was at one of these gatherings, Jolt greeted me with an introduction: 'Here's Harry: he've come over from Hickling purpose to sing to you tonight.' Thus it was I first met Harry Cox, still in his prime today, and probably unique in England as a folk singer, presenting his songs with true artistry in a style which has almost disappeared. The Cox's have been musicians and singers for generations, and Harry has such a prodigious memory that, apart from his large repertory of songs handed down through the family, he is capable of hearing, on no more than three or four separate occasions, a song of a dozen or more verses and remembering it permanently.

These public-house sing-songs, or 'frolics' in local parlance, led to opportunities of meeting and hearing many other songsters. They also led to a friendly rivalry on the part of some of them as to who could contribute the most songs to my collection. Even if a song was one already known, or possibly not a folk song at all, I found it expedient to pretend to be noting it, in order not to cause offence. For one evening Jolt had stopped dead halfway through a song and, in spite of shouts of encouragement from the assembled company, 'Go you on, old Bob, you're a'doing,' he refused to sing another note. 'No, I ain't a'goin on', he said, 'He ain't a'writin on it down in his book.'

64

It seems likely that the spontaneous singing of old songs when men foregather on Saturday nights has now died out.

In this account of some of my experiences of English folk-singing I have not been concerned with the artificial revival of the art. In other words, with those who set about the teaching of folk-songs in schools, or the organising of garden fêtes etc, at which folk-songs are sometimes performed in the highly sophisticated manner of those who have never heard a real traditional singer. Well-intentioned as these efforts may be, they evolve something quite apart from the art of those who have it in their very bones, handed down from father to son. It is unfortunate, too, that up to the present the verbal text of nearly all published collections of English folk-songs bear about the same relationship to the genuine article as does Thomas Bowdler's version to the authentic Shakespeare. It is to be hoped that some day this may be remedied by a complete edition of the country's heritage of song, in which nothing worthwhile is glossed over or left out for reasons of squeamishness or timidity.

Jack's description of how he was able to collect folk-songs from simple country people emphasises one of his most endearing qualities — his ability to gain confidence and respect from those who were close to Nature. In his obituary article, quoted at the end of this book, Sir Arnold Bax also comments on this gift of Jack's. I myself, on several occasions witnessed how he behaved when we visited pubs in Bucks. After getting our mugs of ale, I would follow him across the bar parlour and sit down near some elderly 'locals'. Before long Jack would get into earnest conversation with them, and it was amazing to see the pleasure on their faces. Being completely without pomposity he was able to share their language and thoroughly enjoy their company.

On November 18th I was at the Central Hall for the fifth Delius concert and met Jack in the interval once again. The programme contained several works that he had not heard before, including some of which he had expressed slight disapproval in one of his early letters.

Over a drink I remember asking him what he thought of the concert, and his reply was, 'Marvellous!. How on earth did Fenby get those works down on paper?' He was referring to pieces dictated to Fenby such as *Songs of Farewell*.

'Well, Jack,' I said, 'Do you still think Delius had written himself out by 1913, as you once said?'

'Hmm, I must admit there was plenty of life left in the old chap at the end', he replied, and left me with the distinct impression that the whole concert, which covered music composed between 1880–1931, had been a revelation to him.

That evening I went home to the country in a blissful mood. And so another year came to an end, with much to remember about a friendship with an unusual and endearing personality.

* * * * *

1947 began with a phone call from Jack on January 3rd, when he asked me to lunch at Swiss Cottage on the 6th, on which day snow began to fall. The next few days were to be the coldest for 76 years and the week-end turned out to be the coldest in living memory.

In early February I bought my first car since before the war, a 1938 Austin Seven Cabriolet. I mention this because Jack was to have many rides in her during the next three years.

On Sunday February 9th Jack did a broadcast in a programme called 'Music Lover's Diary', in which he spoke about folk-music.

There is no doubt that Jack's music was getting reasonable exposure during this period. On February 23rd his *Sinfonietta* was broadcast, conducted by Anthony Bernard.

The first week of March was marked by thick snow — and no news of Jack's whereabouts; but on the 20th I sent him a copy of *The Gramophone* magazine in which I had written an article on Moeran and his music (see appendix A).

I sent this magazine to Kington but did not receive his usual prompt reply, so assumed he was in Eire. In fact there was complete silence from Jack and Peers until June 1st, when I received a letter from the latter:

> 55 Belsize Lane,
> N.W.3.

Dear Lionel,

Do you think you could pop in and see this good woman on my behalf and that of my Quartet. I enclose the dope but, as you know, a personal touch does more than any correspondence.

> Maybe I shall blow in on you. Jack's still away and God knows when the Hell he is coming back. The Cello Sonata will be at 6.30. June 5th. I'm off to Dublin to play there.

> Best wishes to all the family,
> Peers

The commision I carried out for Peers was to interview a daily woman, and if possible to engage her. She turned out to be of Irish extraction and for better or worse I took her on.

Peers was so busy at this period, and was often away for days at a time; a housekeeper of some kind had therefore become a necessity. She had also joined the Fitzgibbon String Quartet, which further occupied her time.

This letter from Peers is very expressive of her mannish way of speaking, and is significant in another respect about which I shall have more to say later on.

The next letter came from Jack himself:

> The Rectory,
> Ledbury.
> August 4th 1947.
>
> My dear Lionel,
> We have been here for the past ten days; things haven't been too good, as we have both been on Doctor's hands. Peers had an accident to her right shoulder trying to move the car when the starter failed to work, and I am getting over a sunstroke of nearly a week ago.
>
> As for Peers, I hope she will soon be alright as she is booked to play the cello on Television August 20th. She is having daily massage treatment, but can scarcely touch her cello this week.
>
> We go to Sussex on Saturday: I have to come up for my Piano Rhapsody which is on the Friday, August 15th Prom. The rehearsals are Thursday (14th) afternoon and Friday morning.
>
> I don't know how you're fixed at home, but I was wondering if I could perhaps come to see you for the night of the 14th if you have by any chance a spare bed that night. Do you think I could?
>
> Dick Jobson was here yesterday: we went out to some uplands looking on the Malvern Hills, very beautiful and secluded but quite different, of course, to Radnor.
>
> The weather has been very good since we came here.
> Best wishes to all,
> Jack

They both seem to have been under the weather, for Peers an especially anxious time just before her recital on television.

Of course I wrote to Jack, saying 'Come by all means for the night of the 14th.'

How he must have enjoyed that trip to the uplands with Dick. Peers was with them, and it was on this occasion that Dick took the splendid photo of them (see page 81), with their backs to us, gazing out to the Malvern Hills — Jack leaning his elbows on a stone pillar, and his attitude expressive of rapt contemplation. This vivid photo was used on the Lyrita record of the Cello Concerto.

August 8th brought a postcard in immediate reply to my letter:

> Ledbury,
>> August 7th.
> Thanks for your letter; we are not going to Sussex till Tuesday. I am glad you can put me up for Thursday. I will ring you up as you suggest, but please send a card here by return with the telephone number of your office.
>> Best wishes to all,
>> Jack.

He already had my office number, given to him several times, but how typical of Jack this was!

In the event he came to stay for August 13th *and* 14th and left before mid-day on the 15th to go to London to hear the piano *Rhapsody* being played that evening at the Proms. Unfortunately I was unable to go with him, but heard the concert over the radio.

During this visit I offered to play my records of Warlock's *The Curlew*, surely the saddest music ever written. Jack would have none of it. Over the years I had noticed his reluctance to talk about Warlock, at one time a very close friend of his. This gifted composer's tragic suicide had left a deep scar on Jack's memory.

Immediately after the concert, Jack and Peers went down to the cottage in Sussex which they had the use of during that summer, and from which he sent a hastily written note:

> The Wattles,
>> Pilt Down,
>>> Nr. Uckfield.
> Dear Lionel,
> Here we are after a safe journey last night, 11 p.m. ex. Victoria, Haywards Heath first stop, then eleven mile drive in the Hornet and were in bed and turned out the light at 12.40 a.m. — pretty good going considering this is in the heart of Sussex.
>> I so enjoyed visiting you again and look forward to seeing you on Sunday.
>> Yours,
>> Jack.
> P.S. Here is the studio key.

Jack's reference to a key concerned a retreat he had found in London. This studio I was to frequent and get to love during the next twelve months. It was situated near Swiss Cottage tube station, and stood hidden by trees at the bottom of a large garden belonging to No. 13 Harben Road, since demolished. This imposing house was owned by Frederick Jackson, renowned chorus-master of the London Philharmonic Choir. He had lent Jack this retreat in which to compose.

When Jack kindly suggested that I have a key to this rural studio in which to do some piano practice in my lunch hour, I agreed with gratitude, for I had been using studios above a shop in the vicinity of my office, where the pianos left much to be desired. Both these venues were handy for my office, where I ran a building firm.

So with Jack's key in my pocket I set out to find this studio. The main house was easy enough to trace, but I had some difficulty in spotting the studio, for it proved to be hidden at the far end of a large garden, access being gained by a pleasant walk along a gravel path flanked by shady trees. It was indeed a 'rural' setting for Jack's composition.

When I entered this charming building for the first time I was enchanted with the cosy, lived-in feel of the place. Dominating the room was a Bechstein grand piano. On the left a settee stood against the wall under the only window. A pretty brick fireplace took up most of the wall opposite the door, on the hearth of which stood a gas fire. A large glass-fronted bookcase was set against the wall to the left of the chimney breast and was full of Jack's music. Several Indian rugs lay on the parquet floor.

I was to spend many happy hours in this sanctum, playing the piano or talking to Jack. I soon fell in love with the grand piano. It was a beautiful instrument, and I had no idea that one day it would be mine.

* * * * *

I have already spoken of Jack's marvellous sense of mimicry. An example of this occurred during his present stay. On the Sunday we both walked up to Seer Green for a drink at the 'Cricketers'. When we came out and were passing the church entrance, Jack began telling me about a chap he had seen who had a most unusual infirmity. This poor fellow's method of walking caused him to rock to and fro, taking two steps forward then one step backward, the net effect being a painfully slow progress in the direction he was trying to go.

Jack was absorbed in the demonstration he was giving me, and seemed bent on walking home in this curious fashion when, to my horror, I noticed that a fascinated audience had gathered outside the church. No doubt this queer figure swaying to and fro, with little forward movement, was an unexpected bonus after a boring sermon.

Betty was just too late to witness Jack's display, the gaping audience and my embarrassment, for by the time she reached us, having come up to tell us that lunch was ready, the demonstration was over.

'Did you have a nice drink?' said Betty.

'Yes, thank you,' replied Jack. 'Purely for medicinal purposes, of course.'

How typical was this reply!

He left us on August 25th. His *Overture for a Masque* was played at the Prom concert that evening.

On September 4th I was lucky enough to find Jack at home in his (I almost said 'our') studio. He was busy at his table, music manuscript spread in all directions.

'Sorry, Jack,' I said, 'You're obviously busy,' but he got up at once and, pushing the tobacco jar forward, he said, 'Come in and sit down.' We sank into the large leather-covered sofa and talked and smoked for a while.

During a brief silence Jack startled me by leaping up and striding across the room to the opposite wall, on which hung an engraving of Schumann. He quickly turned the picture frame face to wall and re-seated himself beside me with a grunt of satisfaction.

'Why did you do that?' I asked.

'Can't stand his music,' he replied.

This vehemently expressed comment was most interesting, because Schumann was a favourite composer of Britten and Jack did not like the latter's music either. I remember walking through the beech woods near Woodfield in 1945 when Jack took my arm and said confidentially, 'I went to see the first performance of *Peter Grimes* last night.'

'Did you?' I replied. 'What did you think of it?'

'It's the music of a shit!' he hissed in my ear.

It was during this meeting at the studio that he played his new

70

Symphony to me on the piano. I can still see the short score in his neat pencil notation. It was in the key of E flat.

'As in Elgar's Second,' said Jack quietly.

It began vigorously with high-flying trumpets, followed by syncopated strings *divisi* – the instrumentation was visible on the score. Even on the piano it was breath-taking in its sweep, and I thought, 'This will out-do the First Symphony if it continues like this.'

I cannot recall how much of the work had been written, but I do remember what fine music it was. It is a tragedy that it was never finished.

Another incident occurs to me in connection with this work. One day a few months previously Jack and I were out for a walk at Jordans when he said, 'I'd like your advice. I'm having a lot of trouble with my new Symphony, and its nearly driving me bats.' Taken aback, I wondered what an amateur like me could possibly offer by way of advice. But I said 'Fire away, Jack.' 'Well,' he said, 'It's the form of the work that worries me; the three movements don't cohere, so to speak – there's a lack of unity between them which is, to my mind, artistically unsatisfying.'

I thought for a minute and then said, 'Couldn't you make a one-movement work of it, Jack, like the Sibelius 7th?' We walked on in silence. I gave him a sidelong glance and saw he was deep in thought.

'Um-m-m,' was the only reply I got, but he was obviously weighing up the idea.

Nothing more was said on this subject until he played the work to me that day in the studio. I cannot remember whether Jack had begun to draw the three movements together, but I feel that he died with the problem unsolved.

I have heard to my great consternation that the unfinished score is in Australia, left by Peers to the Victoria College. All Jack's manuscripts should reside in the country of his birth, which he loved so much and which was the inspiration for all his music.

Meanwhile, I have corresponded with a musicologist in Australia, who confirms that the Second Symphony and other manuscripts do indeed exist out there, and that he is orchestrating the 17 pages of the former. Among the manuscripts is an Overture in short score, and sketches of some songs.

This is a most welcome developement which may enable us to hear Jack's final efforts at composition. Judging by what I heard that day in the studio I know that the Symphony would prove a rewarding experience.

It was on this same visit that he gave me his large score of Debussy's *Pelléas et Mélisande*, which I still treasure.

One other incident connected with the studio is very clear in my memory, though not directly to do with Jack. One day I was leaving the studio after some piano practice when a man approached me down the garden path.

'Been playing on Jack's Bechstein?' he enquired.

'Yes', I replied, shifting my music from one arm to the other.

'May I see?' he asked, and I handed over the scores, which he quickly glanced through.

'Ah, you like Delius?' he said. 'Come into the music room,' and he led the way up some wide steps giving access to the French windows of a large high-ceilinged room in the main house.

So far my new acquaintance had offered no clue as to who he was, but I guessed that he must be Frederick Jackson, owner of the whole property.

Sitting down at a full-sized grand piano he said, 'Remember this?' and began to play an excerpt from Delius' *Mass of Life*, softly humming the vocal parts. It was an experience I have never forgotten, for this man's memory was prodigious and his feeling for the music intense. He told me that he always enjoyed coaching his choir for this work, and that they had performed it several times.

I told Jack about this experience, and he was genuinely envious — 'How I wish I'd been there, he's a great choir-trainer,' he said.

Our family was about to go to Felpham, in Sussex, for a fortnight's holiday, and Betty and I thought that Jack and Peers might like to stay at Woodfield while we were away. They leapt at this idea, and on September 7th they motored down to see us off and take possession. They agreed to look after Chippy and Micky, our two dogs, who seemed resigned to their fate.

Before we set out Jack gave me a very welcome gift — the score of his *Sinfonietta*.

* * * * *

When we returned it was obvious that they had enjoyed themselves, and were looking well and happy. I noticed some manuscript standing on the piano and took a quick look at it. The score was headed *Serenade for Orchestra*. Jack later told me that in this new work he was using some material from an earlier two-piano suite.

The *Serenade* was to receive its première during the 1948 Proms.

Jack was full of amusing incidents that had occurred at Woodfield in our absence. As usual, he had noticed any oddity about either the tradesmen calling at the door or people he had seen during their walks around Jordans. Some of the latter people were well-known to us, of course, so we could fully appreciate his uncanny mimicry. As usual, the children were delighted.

Jack was much amused by a habit of our dog Micky, who they nicknamed 'The Human Dustbin' because of the way he waited in ambush until Peers had thrown food to the chickens, whereupon, judging the coast to be clear, he would steal the lot!

* * * * *

The next time we saw them both was on October 19th, when they motored down for the day. I was able to show Jack my new 'OO' gauge model railway layout that was beginning to take shape in the back bedroom, where in the past he used to go to view passing trains. The track ran round this room on a baseboard fixed to trestles, and was beginning to look quite realistic. Jack was naturally fascinated, and I had difficulty in tearing him away when Betty said tea was ready. What an endearing companion he could become!

While we were enjoying ourselves upstairs, Peers was talking in a frank manner to Betty about her relationship with Jack. She told my wife that 'It was like living with an uncle − you don't know how frustrated I feel.'

The reader will know that we had already sensed that things were not quite as they should have been between them. For some time we had felt that they behaved more like brother and sister, accentuated by Peers' tom-boyish and forthright manner. Jack's was a reserved nature, and he seldom showed his feelings, but even so Betty and I were intuitively sure that the marriage was a curious one, and not helped by constant separation due to Peers' many playing engagements at home and abroad. Jack was very much a lone spirit yet restless in his habits, but I still think that if he and Peers could have settled down in the country there might have been more happiness for both of them, and a greater likelihood of regular composition from Jack.

The last three years of his life were to gain a momentum of tragedy which we all seemed powerless to prevent. There were only two major works and a few songs to come now; and in the background was his constant worry over the recalcitrant Second Symphony — and ever-present strain on a gradual mental recession.

* * * * *

I called in at Jack's studio on October 22nd to do some piano practice and was glad to find him in residence. He had the knack of making one feel welcome, and I was seldom at a loss to find matters to discuss — music and railways mostly. He loved to be argumentative, but I was used to that and wouldn't have wished it otherwise. He often stated opinions as facts, only to completely change position later on! A good example of this endearing trait was his dismissal of certain works of Delius (see his early letters to me). After we had known him for a few years I noticed that he would let slip a favourable comment about some of these 'bad works'. But to my chagrin he never withdrew his regard for Delius's Piano Concerto — a subject we often discussed.

I had lunch with him in town on December 1st. We dropped in at a pub off Regent Street where musicians could usually be found. On this occasion we met Parry Jones, the tenor, who was standing at the bar wearing a black sombrero hat; we chatted with him about his recent song recitals.

One evening in December I picked up Jack in the Austin Seven at Marylebone. It was dark by then, and as we made our way along Western Avenue he was quietly recovering from his recent visit to the bar at the station, and quite happy to just sit and dream with his pipe.

As I have mentioned, Jack had a 'gammy' leg which, when he sat down, he thrust out before him. This was now the case that evening in the Austin, and leg-room was very restricted in that cosy little car.

When we were passing Gerrards Cross Common there was an ear-splitting sound of cracking metal, and the back of Jack's seat collapsed, causing him to assume a horizontal posture with his head on the back seat! Much alarmed I called out,

'Are you all right, Jack?'

'Yes', came a muffled reply from somewhere in the rear. 'Carry on'. He remained in that position until we got home, where I had great difficulty in extricating him; I expected some comment on the affair, but none was forthcoming.

Jack's stiff leg had been the cause of a more serious accident a few years previously. Apparently he was staying with Robert Nichols, the poet, when during a gramophone session Jack thrust forward his stiff leg and sat down heavily on the couch. There was an appalling sound of breakage, and leaping up Jack was horrified to see that he had ruined a seven-record set of Beethoven Piano Sonatas played by Artur Schnabel. The horror he had experienced by this event was still present as he narrated the incident.

Anyway, during this visit I was able to let Jack hear a new set of records which I had just had privately made. This was *The Hills* by Patrick Hadley, and was the first performance of the work, recently given at the Proms. I admired Hadley's music and knew that he was an old friend of Jack's, and that they had a mutual passion for railways: so, handing him my score of the work, I started the gramophone and sat down to watch his reaction to the music. I remember so well the little secret smile that came and went as the music developed − as if he kept recognising familiar landmarks. At the end he remained quiet for a moment, still smiling, and said, 'I enjoyed that − very much.' I was not surprised by this remark as both composers were half Irish; both were inspired by Nature and had a mutual regard for Delius. Indeed, Hadley had once stated that the latter's *Song of the High Hills* was his favourite piece of music.

It is interesting that Jack held Dvorak in high esteem. 'It's outdoor music of the finest kind', he said.

* * * * *

The next letter was the last to be received that year, and was very typical:

Ledbury,
31/12/47.

Dear Lionel,

I have changed my plans and am not coming back for a brief spell in London but am going straight off to Ireland, starting from here tonight. The fact is, the B.B.C. date for collecting songs in Co. Kerry had been put forward, and as I want to do some work on my own account at the same time, it seems better and, at the same time, far cheaper as to fare, to push on from here.

I think you might like to use my studio to practise in, so I will send the key thereof. Use it as much as you can, and the more you use my piano in my absence, the better for it.

I was rather rushed coming away before Christmas and I remember that I clean forgot to do up and post the signal-box for Nicholas. You will find it's component parts in the cupboard in a cardboard box on the right where music is kept, so please take it home with you and it may come for Nick as a belated savour of Christmas.

In the meantime my address is: –

The Lodge,
Kenmare,
Co. Kerry, Eire.

Please do not use the oil-stove as I am not sure of it yet; it is quite a new one. You can get all the gas you want for a shilling to the meter. It will be well for the piano if you light the gas fire as often as possible.

Best wishes to all for 1948,
Jack

He must have forgotten that I already had the studio key, and he knew that I practised there when he was away!

I well remember finding his forgotten present for Nicholas, and the latter's pleasure when he opened this kind, if tardy, gift.

It has probably occurred to the reader that nothing that Jack said or did ever surprised me, and this was largely true. But of recent months I had noticed that he was becoming a bit vague and forgetful at times. Being a gradual process it did not unduly worry me; so the business of two keys for the studio caused no more than an amused smile at the time. But one must bear this trend in mind as the last period unfolds.

* * * * *

Jack Moeran

Albert Sammons in 1944

*Above: Jack Moeran
with Lionel Hill and
his son Nicholas.*

*Jack Moeran in 1943
on the railway bank
at Woodfield.*

Peers Coetmore

Above: Peers Coetmore in Piccadilly.
Below: Peers and Jack in the Malvern Hills,
*   photographed by his friend Dick Jobson.*

*Above: Jack Moeran and Peers Coetmore on their wedding day, 1945.
Below: Setting off on honeymɔon.*

Jack Moeran in 1948

Above: Mount Melleray Abbey, County Waterford
Below: The quay at Kenmare, where Moeran died.

It is sad to realize that only two years remained of Jack's companion-ship. We had seen a lot of him during the previous twelve months, but I had no inkling of how short our time together was to be.

* * * * *

We did not see Jack again until June 28th. Early in the 1948 he went over to Eire, to his beloved Kenmare, his spiritual home. The older he became the greater was the upsurge of his Irish ancestry. It was something very deep in his subconscious, for he spoke and behaved like a typical English public school product of his generation. Indeed, Sir Arnold Bax in his obituary article stated that for the first 30 years of his life Jack was an Englishman, and a diligent collector of East Anglian folk-tunes, whilst for the remainder of his life he was almost exclusively Irish.

Meanwhile, I was daily practising at Jack's studio in Harben Road, and becoming increasingly fond of his Bechstein Grand. Eventually it occurred to me that he might be willing to sell it, so I wrote to him, asking his opinion on this idea.

Back came a telegram: –

> Kenmare,
> 1/3/48.
> Willing sell Bechstein piano if suitable for your reasonable price.
> Jack

This was good news. Luckily I had already met Jack's piano-tuner at the studio, a dear old gentleman called Mr Pevier, so I quickly arranged for him to vet the piano. He knew the instrument well, and said that it required re-stringing and re-felting and gave his opinion as to its value.

I passed on this information to Jack but received no reply to my letter until March 12th, when I got both a telegram and a letter. The former read:

> Kenmare,
> March 11th 1948.
> Did you get my wire accepting your proposal.
> Have also written.

I never received that telegram! The letter was more helpful:

                    The Lodge,
                    Kenmare.
                        11/3/48.
Dear Lionel,
I have to write in a hurry also (I will send you a long letter later), but I can't make out if you had my last wire.

Anyway, I would like you to have the piano if it appeals to you.

If Pevier says £150 is fair, I am sure he would not be letting either of us down.

I wired you saying let Pevier go ahead, but this was some days ago, so I wonder if you got it.

Anyway, that will suit me so long as you don't think I am swindling you, but it's a lovely instrument once it's had a bit of renovation.
                    Yours as ever,
                    Jack
P.S. New E Flat Symphony going strong.

It was so typical of Jack to wonder whether he was being over-paid. I remember being thrilled to learn that the Symphony was progressing, and wondering if his difficulties with its form structure were receding.

I must have replied at once to Jack's last letter, because he wrote by return:

                    Kenmare,
                    March 12th /48.
My dear Lionel,
Many thanks for your letter and wire. I had to bother you with the wire as I had another offer which I have turned down.

Excuse this awful rush but the post goes out so early here and there is no post at all tomorrow (Sunday). I will write more fully during the week-end with other news.
                    Now I have to dash for post.
                    Jack.

When Betty and I read this letter we sensed that Jack's 'another offer' was born in the Celtic mists of S.W. Eire! We knew our Jack by now, and were quite willing to accept such idiosyncrasy; it was a part of the joy of knowing him.

                    * * * * *

86

On March 18th, Jack sent an intriguing letter:

> The Lodge,
> Kenmare.
>
> My Dear Lionel,
>
> As I had told you, my last letter was in a hurry as I had to catch the post in reply to yours.
>
> The enclosed cutting from *The Scotsman* of February 12th will no doubt make you very annoyed; it is slighly old history, however only a month or so; it was sent me by an old Edinburgh friend. Perhaps you would feel disposed to write to Mr. Deas, who is the perpetrator of it.
>
> There are one or two points: − (a) Is Sir Thomas Beecham such a fool as to have for years championed the cause of tripe!? (b) That Delius only meanders about in chords. How about the tremendous fugal chorus in *The Mass of Life*? This work is full of counterpoint elsewhere. (c) As for vamping about the keyboard, his last works, including the *Songs of Farewell*, were written by dictation.
>
> However, you may think of a lot more to say. I am too busy to enter into controversies.
>
> This Symphony is the devil of a job: I shall get it done in time, but the question of form and construction is causing me some trouble, as I am arriving at a single-movement work, or rather a continuous piece having the ingredients of the usual movements.
>
> As for hearing music, I am very much cut off here, as being in such a mountainous country, and at sea level into the bargain, radio transmission is very poor, but when trying to compose on a major scale, it is perhaps as well to be cut off from outside influences.
>
> But if I am not back for the production of Vaughan Williams' new Symphony, I must get somewhere where it will be possible to listen-in to it if it is broadcast. I could perhaps go to Cork for a night, where listening-in conditions are good.
>
> You should have little difficulty in disposing of your upright piano as they are surely in great demand these days. Thank you for mentioning that you are arranging for the cheque now. I do hope this is not inconvenient to you but, strictly between ourselves, I find I have made a bad calculation in going over accounts as to my financial state, so I am really in need of some money at the moment. I never was any good at figures and money matters and, whereas I thought I had a good balance in the bank, I find I was mistaken. But not a word to anybody, Peers especially, as she is so good at business matters that I like her to think I am not such a complete fool.
>
> Anyhow, I am sure you will be pleased with the piano when the necessary renovations have been attended to. I used to get great joy out of it,

but latterly in that little studio, which is too small for it, I have preferred my Bechstein upright, which I have here.

I have a few formalities to deal with about getting it to England, e.g. written corroboration that it belongs to me. I shall have to go up to Cork and see a friend at the Customs.

I did not know that Furtwangler had appeared in London yet. When I heard him before the War I thought he was not very good, not a patch on Weingartner for example. In fact I thought he was somewhat of a charlatan.

Things are coming out well — plenty of daffodils, primroses, rhododendrons etc:. The hedges are turning green, but the trees are still backward.

I expect Peers in two weeks time.

Best wishes to all,
Jack

I read and re-read this letter: it contained so many confidences.

Unfortunately I no longer have the cutting from *The Scotsman* that caused Jack so much indignation, but evidently Mr Deas had indulged in a bitter attack against Delius. I don't recall taking up the cudgels, but Jack's displeasure was good news in itself.

His reference to the new Symphony was both interesting and disquietening. It was evidently still giving him trouble, in spite of the fact that he seemed to have adopted my previous suggestion for a one-movement work.

The new Symphony of Vaughan Williams must have been the Sixth. It would be like Jack to make every effort to hear a new work by one of his three favourite composers.

What a cry from the heart was his admission of being unable to manage money matters!

His remarks about Furtwangler were in answer to my information that this famous conductor was giving concerts in London.

At the end of March I sent Jack my cheque for the piano, which he immediately acknowledged by wire.

The following day he sent a letter:

Kenmare,
April 2nd 1948.

My dear Lionel,

I couldn't write before, as I was away in Cork meeting Peers. Anyway, thank you for the cheque, which I have sent to my London bank. However, so that you would know I had it safe and sound, I sent a wire yesterday.

I am very grateful to you for what you say about going to the Hallé concert with Albert (to whom my very best wishes and undying gratitude for what he made of my work in absolutely re-creating it as he did at Norwich).

Now, as regards those discs, I am most awfully sorry, but Peers will still be here on April 13th and they are all put away where they can't be got at.

Honestly, I can't see that there is anything to be done about it. What a pity you didn't get the chance of seeing Peers before she left last week.

We have the use of a Ford Prefect which goes alright, but is a bit tricky, as you have to hold your hand fast in second.

The weather is pretty bad. It has been lovely, but it has gone and played the same trick on Peers as it did last time she was here.

Love and greetings to all from us both,
Jack

Albert Sammons' performance of the Violin Concerto had undoubtedly impressed Jack, and now more than ever we both prayed that a recording might be made.

In early April I wrote again to Barbirolli, enclosing a copy of *The Gramophone* in which appeared an article of mine on Moeran. I told him that this magazine had published many readers' letters requesting a recording of the Concerto.

I received the following reply:

The Hallé Concerts Society,
Manchester.
April 13th 1948.
Dear Mr. Hill,
Mr. Barbirolli has asked me to thank you for your kind letter of the 7th, also for the copy of *The Gramophone*. He has already read your excellent article, in which he was greatly interested.

He was most gratified to learn of the interest shown by readers of your article on the Moeran Violin Concerto, and would, as you know, be really delighted to be able to take part in a recording of this work. However, despite repeated representations to the Gramophone Company about this, nothing has been done. You may rest assured that Mr. Barbirolli has done all in his power to try to bring about a recording which would give him very much pleasure indeed.

Mr. Barbirolli has asked me to convey to you his best wishes.
Yours sincerely,
Sidney Rothwell,
Secretary to Mr. Barbirolli.

So the prospect for a recording within the near future did look bleak. Indeed, not until 1979 was the work recorded, by John Georgiadis with the London Symphony Orchestra conducted by Vernnon Handley. Thirty-two years were to elapse before such an event took place. It is incredible that such a lovely work should have been neglected by the recording companies for so long.

The Bechstein was delivered to Woodfield on April 22nd, and stood in our spacious living room looking every bit the aristocrat it was.

A few days previously I had written to Jack asking his permission to store our upright piano temporarily at his studio, and received the following wire in reply:

> Kenmare,
> 13/4/48
> Certainly use studio for your upright piano.
> Jack

So this course of action was taken, and the lorry returned to London with our upright.

The following day Pevier came to tune the grand. Luckily Jack had warned us about a disconcerting habit that Pevier had of tuning a piano not only with his ears but also with the help of a nose-bleed! Sure enough, that excellent old craftsman produced a copious bleed, but he always left everything clean and tidy. This habit of Pevier's fascinated Jack.

Laurence Turner, leader of the Hallé, broadcast the Violin Concerto on April 27th, and Peers gave a recital at the Wigmore Hall on May 12th, which I was unable to attend.

On June 4th I wrote to Jack, after which he must have returned to England for I had lunch with him on June 28th and heard all his news.

The next time we met was at the studio on July 16th — my upright piano looking strange after the Bechstein.

Jack came down to Woodfield for the day on Sunday July 25th. He was most interested to see and play on his old grand, and thought Pevier had done a superb job on it. During the evening he sat at the Bechstein and played through my score of Delius' *Requiem*. 'There's some gorgeous music in that', he said: 'Why is it never performed?'

It was during this visit that Jack told us of his intention to look for a rural retreat in Bucks. We thought this was a marvellous idea; it would

90

be good for him, he would be near us, and we could perhaps keep him away from the bad influence of some of the 'friends' in town. So we fixed the next week-end for him.

When Jack arrived on July 31st his first words were, 'I've heard of a cottage at a place called Radnage, not far from here; perhaps we could go and look at it tomorrow?' Of course we agreed at once, and the next day set out in the Austin Seven, Jack puffing at his pipe and studying a map with the utmost concentration.

We eventually found Radnage by climbing high on the Chilterns, where a magnificent view opened out before us. We were on Bledlow Ridge. The cottage lay well back from the road in an isolated position, and as we walked towards it I thought 'What could be better than this!' The owner showed us round what seemed to be a separate wing with its own staircase.

'Oh Lord,' exclaimed Jack, 'I'll never get my piano up those narrow stairs!'

I saw his point, so we took a few measurements and found to our dismay that no piano would reach the first floor of that cottage — and the ground floor did not form a part of the lease. In fact, Jack's quarters would have been what was the attic.

This one snag spoilt what could have been an ideal pied-à-terre for Jack, and we returned home in a very dejected mood.

I have mentioned before Jack's singular rapport with country folk, and we were treated to another example of this facet of his character on the return journey from Chinnor.

We had brought the perquisites for a picnic, and found a suitable field in which to set up the primus stove, etc, when a burly farmer appeared and angrily told us to be off. Jack got up and said quietly, 'Leave this to me'. He strolled towards the irate figure and we watched them talking for a while. I was not surprised to see the farmer's expression relax, nor to receive his permission to proceed with our picnic, for I had seen Jack in action with country people on several occasions, noting his complete ease with them. I have seen nothing like it before or since.

During this visit Jack and I heard two works over the wireless which gave him much pleasure. John Ireland's major piano suite *Sarnia* had only just been published, and neither of us had heard it before. Jack was intensely moved by this atmospheric depiction of the Channel

Islands. The other work was Shostakovitch's First Symphony. Jack said, 'He was only eighteen when he wrote that, and I don't think he's written anything better so far'.

Also during that stay occurred a memorable session with the gramophone. After supper on the Sunday I was able to surprise Jack with the news that I had just bought the newly released records of Delius' opera *A Village Romeo and Juliet*. 'Oh, do let's hear it!' he said, and sank into the sofa with our dog Chippy on his lap.

I set the gramophone going. Jack lit his pipe and leaned back, gazing at the ceiling, his hands gently caressing the dog. As the lovely opera unfolded I noticed that he was becoming more and more restless, clouds of smoke coming from his pipe. I knew instinctively that he would not be able to contain himself much longer, and when the beautiful music of the love scene engulfed us he was so moved that he leapt to his feet, flinging the bewildered dog to the floor, and paced to and fro, repeatedly muttering 'What's the use, it's all been done before! All said better already.' Never before had I seen Jack like this. It was an experience I have never forgotten.

How much Jack was influenced by Delius is a matter for argument, but after that evening we knew beyond doubt how deeply he could be moved by this composer.

Jack left on August 2nd and the following week came a postcard: —

> Ledbury
> August 11th/48
>
> My piano is in London. I wonder if yours has had any offers, because I have got to get mine in to Harben Road. It is just possible with yours, only an awful squash. But don't forget I have got to move out all furniture at the end of the month. We return to Belsize Lane tomorrow, so will ring you Friday morning at the office.
>
> Hope you enjoyed last night at the Proms, but if you had train to catch you may have missed Haydn's Concertante, apart from *Appalachia*, the best work on the programme.
> E.J.M.

Jack evidently went to stay with his brother for a day or so at Ledbury.

* * * * *

The family went on holiday to Felpham again between August 23rd and September 5th, from where I wrote to Jack telling him that we had just had lunch with Norman Demuth, the composer and musicologist, who wished to be remembered to him.

During this holiday a new work of Jack's was given its première at the Proms: this was the *Serenade* for orchestra on which he had worked during his stay at Woodfield the previous year. The conductor was Basil Cameron.

I had a private recording made of this performance which has turned out to be most valuable, because when this work came to be published by Novello it was considered to be too long. Two movements were omitted and will never be heard again, except on my record.

While at Felpham I received a letter from Peers' studio:

> 55 Belsize Lane,
> August 25th
>
> Dear Lionel,
> Many thanks for the cheque.
>
> I was on the Oxford road yesterday and intended turning off at Seer Green when I remembered you were away. I went to Chinnor: the house there in the woods is ideal for work if I can solve the problem of getting some meals.
>
> I left the car at Gerrards Cross, coming back, and caught train to Marylebone.
>
> It is being generally gone over, head tightened down, tappets adjusted and various oddments, of which I gave Davies a list, after 700 miles running-in.
>
> Peers is on an Arts Council tour in Yorkshire and I hear that she is having great success and they want her to go again.
>
> I am going to the Prom tonight to hear Rawsthorne's Concerto and Elgar's *Falstaff*.
>
> It must be lovely by the sea now. We are having high winds here but it is warm. Yesterday was a heavenly day in Bucks.
>
> > Best wishes to all,
> > Jack
>
> P.S. My piano arrived in almost perfect tune! No need for Pevier till after I move. It is a great old war-horse.

The projected house at Chinnor failed to materialize, though I do not recall why this second abortive attempt by Jack to find peace and quiet in the country failed.

There is no doubt that things were now becoming desperate. He had lost the studio in Harben Road; the Belsize Lane studio was too noisy and frequented by Peers' friends. There was Kington of course, to which he went for a few days at intervals, but there must have been reasons which prevented him from staying there for long at a time and really getting down to composition.

I think now, looking back over thirty years, that Jack found himself in a cleft stick. He was married to someone who found relations with him difficult, and who for several reasons was not in a position to make a proper home for him. In any case, Jack had always been used to complete freedom — it was vital to him. He had spent most of his life in the country — Norfolk, Herefordshire, Kerry, etc., with short visits to town only when absolutely necessary. Every note of his music had been inspired by contact with Nature, and without that stimulus he was a lost spirit.

* * * * *

On September 8th Jack gave a talk on the Third Programme, the sixth of a series called 'Musical Curiosities'.*

It was to be a long while before we would see him again, for he went over to Eire in the first week of October, and complete silence reigned for the rest of the year.

* * * * *

It is somewhat more difficult to sum up the previous twelve months than in recent years. Our friendship with Jack was as strong as hitherto, but gone were the days and happy times when he came to Woodfield so frequently. With hindsight one can see that his creative ability was beginning to falter, and tragically was not to recover. The beautiful Atlantic seaboard and Celtic spirit of Kenmare were claiming him for their own with ever-increasing intensity, and would before long keep him for ever.

The first five weeks of 1949 were to pass without a sight of Jack, but a letter came in February with news that he was staying in Cheltenham: —

---

* This was a monthly series in which music ans such as Rene Soames, the BBC Singers, Stewart Wilson, Constant Lambert and others took part.

94

Park House West,
Cheltenham
February 4th 1949

Dear Betty and Lionel,

I see in the Radio Times that my Symphony is on at Albert Hall next Wednesday night. I see so little of you these days that I am wondering if possibly I could come to Seer Green the previous night (Tuesday) and catch the 8.10 up to London on Wednesday morning for rehearsal. Don't hesitate to say if inconvenient.

I had an airmail letter card from Peers today, posted at Port Said. She was not going ashore, being down with flu, of which they have an epidemic on board.

Yours sincerely,
Jack

Good news at last! We were going to see him again, and on his own, as in happy by-gone times.

The forthcoming performance of the G minor Symphony was to be under the baton of Sir Adrian Boult. I immediately arranged for a private recording to be made.

It was marvellous to see Jack on February 8th when he stayed the night. We thought he somehow looked changed — his eyes were more bloodshot and his face more flabby. He was still as companionable as ever, but Betty and I were filled with a vague foreboding. He was so loyal to Peers and full of admiration for her evidently successful tours, but we felt that he was left on his own too much with no-one to look after him, or keep him away from harmful influences.

Jack and I both thought Boult's rendering of the Symphony to have been a very fine one. I still have the records, made at 78 rpm of course.

March 18th brought Jack to us again, this time for the weekend. Although we did not realize it at the time, this visit would be the last he spent at Woodfield, and the last but one that he would ever stay under our roof. Mercifully lacking this foresight, we spent a very happy weekend, with walks and much discussion on musical topics, and a long session with the model railway. His enthusiasm over this gave me much pleasure.

He told us that the reason for his stay in Cheltenham was to attend the festival concerts, and seemed keen that I should join him there. I said it would hardly be possible as I could not leave my business for so long, but that I would think it over.

The old Jack came to the fore when he was describing his 'digs' in Cheltenham. His landlady had a habit of repeating herself in everything she said, which tickled him immensely. An instance he gave was when she knocked on his door with a morning cup of tea and the announcement: – 'I've brought your cup of tea, Mr. Moeran – I SAY, I'VE BROUGHT YOUR CUP OF TEA.' Jack's mimicry was superb.

* * * * *

Once again several weeks elapsed before hearing any news of him, but from Cheltenham came this letter:

> Park House West,
> Cheltenham
> 9/5/49

Dear Lionel,

I am awfully sorry, but the spare room has been permanently let to a wretched female professor of shorthand.

This means I can't put you up, should you come for the Festival. However, if you mean to come to Cheltenham then, and let me know in good time, I could probably find you sleeping quarters at reasonable terms nearby.

I find I am seriously wanting Albert's recording of my Concerto. Do you think you could get the studio to make a set from your master copy as soon as possible? In which case, I wonder what they would charge.

You might put it to them that I propose going to them in future when I want anything recorded off the air, as I am not by any means satisfied with H's work for me since he left B&H and opened on his own, as he has no direct line and, especially with Third Programme recordings, his results are liable to a lot of interference.

I should be very grateful if you could see to this as soon as it is possibly convenient.

I see the April *Gramophone* has got going again on the subject of recording my Concerto with Albert, but I don't suppose anything is likely to come of it, any more than before.

> Yours,
> Jack

It was kind of Jack to try and get lodgings for me there, but I had to reply that it was impossible for me to join him.

His reference to the *Gramophone* concerned some readers' letters backing up my previous pleas in that paper for a recording of the concerto.

I made enquiries at the studio and found that a copy of the Violin Concerto could be made from my master, so I wrote to Jack quoting the price. As usual his reply was not delayed:

Cheltenham
May 12th 1949
Dear Lionel,
Thanks for your letter. I am most interested to hear about the progress of the railway. I suppose Nicholas is now back at school again.

Please go ahead with the recording and have the discs sent to me here. Shall I send you the £5 to pay for it, or to the studio? Please let me know, but if it isn't putting you to too much trouble, I really need them as soon as possible owing to someone coming here influential with H.M.V., I want to strike while the iron is hot.

I am sorry you can't come for the Festival. After it is over, I must find other quarters, as I shan't be able to stand the summer heat in this flat, which is up in the roof. Moreover, the flue from the furnace heating the hot water for the bathroom and the whole house runs up the sitting room wall, so I have a species of central heating which can't be turned off, as well as the sun beating down on the roof.

I think of trying to find digs in some farmhouse up in the hills in the surrounding country. Moreover, this service flat is more than I can afford financially.

Please tell me Fournier's date at Jordans. I so much want to meet him again. As you say, the wireless programmes have been poor. However, I enjoyed Busoni's Piano Concerto last night.
Yours,
Jack

There is a sad undertone to this letter. The same theme is explicit and gathering momentum — where shall he settle down and find peace? His longing for the country is again evident, and one had a feeling of helplessness; of knowing Jack's problem yet being unable to assist in any positive way.

Of course I put his discs on order without delay. I had told Jack that Pierre Fournier and Francis Poulenc were to give a recital at Jordans on June 18th. A music club had been formed during the war, and many well-known artists took part each year, the concerts taking place in the Mayflower Barn. This old, timber-framed building had been constructed from the remains of the famous ship that took William Penn and his fellow Quakers to America, where they founded Pennsylvania.

I remember appearances at these concerts of Benjamin Britten and Peter Pears, Michael Tippett and his Morley College Choir, Albert Sammons and Kathleen Long, Edmund Rubbra and his wife, Mewton Wood the pianist, and others.

The next letter shows that Jack was still in Cheltenham:

Cheltenham,
May 20th/49

Dear Lionel,

Thanks for your letter and for your trouble over the records. I've sent £5 to the recording studio, and asked them to send them to me here.

I had hopes of seeing you on Wednesday as I was up in London. I had business at Joseph Williams in Enford Street (near Marylebone); they have just published my Overture; I will give you a score when I next see you, or tell them to send you one.

Anyway, I finished with them shortly after 4.30 and it occurred to me to go over to the station and see you for a minute or two in the event of your travelling on the 5.15. (Incidentally, I wanted to do a pumpship, so I had to go to the station in any case). However, there was no sign of you, for which I was sorry.

Thanks for suggesting June 18th. I will let you know later.

A pity Nicholas won't be home then; I should like to hear him play the horn.

All the best to everyone at Woodfield.

Yours,
Jack

P.S. I must definitely contact Heifitz when he plays on Sunday June 5th, so I shall go up to London that week-end.

Note how Jack loved to qualify a statement, for instance, the reason he gave for trying to see me at the station.

We have often thought how interested Jack would have been in Nicholas' career as a French horn player, for he has been a well-known member of his profession for many years, and has played in most of the famous orchestras. Conversely, Nick has often expressed his regret that he was not older during our friendship with Jack.

We were sorry to read in the following letter that he would not be coming to the Fournier concert:

Cheltenham,
June 14th 1949

Dear Lionel,

I am sorry that I cannot avail myself of your kind suggestion for me to come next week-end for Fournier concert but, apart from anything else, I have become very run down as a result of the awful humidity of the Cheltenham climate in the summer, so I am going over tomorrow to New Radnor for a few days to get braced up with some mountain air to be put into good form for the Festival.

I am sending a copy of my Cello Sonata which I should be very grateful if you would hand to Pierre Fournier; explain to him that I would have sent it to him direct, but I don't know his address in England. You will find him very nice and agreeable.

I met Albert at Heifitz's concert. Heifitz got through the Elgar in record time; while realizing his brilliance, I cannot say I admired his interpretation. On the other hand, Fournier's playing of the Cello Concerto was a sheer delight.

All best wishes,
Jack

P.S. I have now got records of Barber's Symphony.

After the concert at Jordans, to which Albert also came, we saw Fournier afterwards and gave him the Cello Sonata, but apart from saying 'Merci' and 'Bon' several times he was obviously at a loss to understand most of what we were trying to say, for he spoke little English. I don't think that this fine cellist ever did play Jack's work.

* * * * *

Shortly after this concert my family was engaged in a major upheaval. For several reasons we decided to sell Woodfield and move to London, and on September 16th we left Bucks for ever.

* * * * *

I met Jack once in London after our move, and told him what had taken place. Like us, he was saddened by this event, but expressed a wish to see our new house.

A few weeks later I received a letter:

                    The Rectory,
                        Ledbury
                            December 27th 1949
Dear Lionel,
I send a cheque for the £10 you so kindly lent me when I was stuck in London.
I would have sent it earlier but for neuritis, which has got me in the most
inconvenient place, namely the right hand, and it is only now after a series
of injections over the past ten days that I am able to do a very little bit of writing.
    Wishing you all a very happy new year,
                    Yours,
                        Jack
P.S. The Ledbury address will find me for the next few weeks.

This letter contained no news about the new Symphony — or of Peers
and her doings.

                        * * * * *

    There is little to sum up about the past year. We had been afforded
a few visits from him, but for most of 1949 he had been in Eire or
Cheltenham. I was completely in the dark with regard to his progress
at composition, and certainly had no inkling of how little time was left.
    It was not until early in January 1950 that we again heard from Jack:

                    The Rectory,
                        Ledbury
                            January 7th 1950
Dear Lionel,
I hate to pester you, but in view of your change of address (I forgot to put
'Please forward'), I am wondering whether you got a letter from me, I think
about a fortnight ago, in which I enclosed a cheque. You did give me your
new address when I saw you in London, but I can't find it.
    I hope you had a good Christmas. My neuritis is very much better, so much
so that I can stretch a tenth on the piano, but I am still having injections.
    Will you be in Town on the 25th when Beecham does my *Sinfonietta*?
I think I must come up for this, in particular to get him if possible to ginger
up the first movement in case he takes to playing the work regularly. Last time
it was a bit too slow, although the rest of the performance was superb.
                    Yours,
                        Jack

This letter was so typical of him in the later years. I was now becoming more worried about his memory. He seemed to forget quite recent events.

We went to hear Beecham conduct the *Sinfonietta* at the Albert Hall, and Jack was staying with us on that occasion. At the end of the performance Beecham turned to face the audience, and with raised head gazed intently around the balcony seats. At length we all spotted Jack sitting in the front row, whereupon Beecham began to clap and everyone followed suit, looking up at the composer, who had turned brick-red and was trying to make himself invisible.

Once again I had a private recording made of this historic performance.

* * * * *

Seven weeks later there came a postcard, which was sadly to prove the last time that the postman would bring a letter or card from Jack:

> The Rectory,
>   Ledbury
>   February 24th 1950
> Under separate cover I am sending you a little Irish tobacco (Wills have an Irish factory). I arrived back Wed: and shall be returning Mar. 6th.
>   I have found a lovely place to live in Co. Wicklow, 17 miles from Dublin. I hope I will see you next week, as I must pay a flying visit to London.
>   J

I remember being very touched by his spontaneous gift, and only wish I had kept the little tin holding the tobacco as a momento; but how was I to know that our last sight of Jack was only a fortnight away?

On March 5th (a day earlier than expected) Jack came to spend the night at our new house in Cricklewood. One or two things about this brief visit stay in my memory — the last time we ever saw him.

He was fascinated by our newly-acquired television set, at which he stared with rapt attention, sitting on the edge of his chair — just as he did when he and I went to see *Sir John in Love*, already described. We had noticed this same posture when, a couple of years previously, we had taken him to the cinema in Beaconsfield to see *Quartet* by Somerset Maugham. I have never seen anyone concentrate with such intensity as Jack.

Of course he insisted on seeing the model railway, and I showed him the new layout that was taking shape in a small bedroom. He was so pleased and interested that I was setting it all up again that my efforts seemed very worthwhile. After Jack's death I lost all heart in this mutual hobby and sold everything.

He also admired our new music room, in which his old Bechstein stood in all its glory.

That evening we played some records, and I remember that Sibelius' Sixth Symphony was one of his choices, also Delius' Cello Sonata, of which he had now become very fond.

At bedtime we put Jack in the little room next to ours, and turning out the light felt that the old happy times were still with us — though Woodfield was a poignant memory.

The next evening we all went to the Albert Hall to hear the Yorkshire Symphony Orchestra play a work of Jack's. At the end we waited for him in the foyer, and noticed a bunch of autograph hunters, who surged forward to intercept him when he at last appeared. It was obvious to us that he had visited the bar after the concert, and as he came towards our group he noticed neither the autograph books thrust forward, nor Betty, Judy and myself. Judy whispered, 'Oh Daddy, I do believe he's squiffy!' But I knew Jack. He never caused trouble when in this condition. I said, 'Not really — just happy,' and hoped she would understand, and pushed my way through the crowd to find him outside looking lost. Taking his arm I beckoned the family and we led him to the car.

He remained quiet and docile all the way home, but just before bedtime he became his old self, and we all retired much relieved.

At breakfast next morning Jack was completely normal, just as he had been when I rescued him from the prickly bushes at Woodfield, six years previously. How he always recovered so quickly is a mystery.

* * * * *

The end of our friendship with Jack was only an hour away. After saying goodbye to Betty and Judy in his usual courteous manner (I shall never forget his politeness on all occasions), he entered the car beside me and we drove to a bus stop in Willesden Lane. On the way he made two remarks, 'I like your new car — and your new house!'

The former was a 1938 15hp Fiat which I had bought just before leaving Woodfield. He only had two rides in her — the trip to the Albert Hall on the previous evening and this short run to the bus stop.

Of course I had no idea that I would never see him again. We were both relaxed and cheerful as we said good-bye. He thanked me again for putting him up, waved, and I drove off to my office.

I can still see him in the driving mirror, standing on the pavement dressed in his tweed coat and cap, looking the countrified Jack we knew so well. I am glad that my last sight of him was so exactly as we shall always remember him.

* * * * *

I have now come to the end of our seven-years friendship with this gifted and lovable man. There were to be no more visits and no more letters. Up to that point he had become so much a part of our lives that the following nine months of complete silence and lack of knowledge as to his whereabouts raised questions to which I can only guess the answers. The last pages of this narrative may provide the reader with clues to partially solve this riddle, but the whole truth may never be known, because most of those who knew Jack are now dead. A future biographer will have little to go upon.

Meanwhile, I think that the letters which form the greater part of this story of our friendship with Jack will speak for themselves.

We received the shock of his sudden death in the morning papers. It was unbelievable. He was seen to fall into the water from Kenmare Pier, and when brought ashore was found to be dead.

It only remains for me to quote from letters I received after Jack's death from his mother, his doctor, Dick Jobson, and the latter's widow. Those from Mrs Moeran senior are especially revealing and poignant, and help to explain the gradual change we had noticed in Jack's appearance and behaviour during the last two years of his life.

Dick Jobson's letters are some of the earliest and show how, as Jack's doctor, he had been worried about him for several years: there are references to 'moods of depression' which, curiously enough, we never experienced. Dick also knew more intimately than we of the failure of his marriage — we only sensed it. Like us, Dick abhorred the bad influence of some of Jack's acquaintances, who took advantage of what they well knew to be his one weakness.

* * * * *

Dick's first letter came within a few months of our happy visit to Kington:

(excerpt)
> The Laurals,
> New Radnor
> 18/12/45

Dear Mr. Hill,

Jack visited me in a state of acute depression some time ago and consented to listen to his Symphony records. I played them to him with the volume well up and he went wild with joy and excitement. It really was a most happy experience.

Incidentally, I suppose you know of his troubles? I had a letter from him this morning and he seems a lot happier now. The Cello Concerto is a great success (I thought the Dublin broadcast topping) and he's at last at work on his second Symphony.

I do hope we shall see you again some day, and that you will come back to Radnor Forest.

I enclose a letter for your father-in-law, a belated appreciation of his playing of Jack's Concerto.

> Yours sincerely,
> Dick Jobson

(excerpt)
> The Laurels,
> New Radnor
> 1/10/46

Dear Mr. Hill,

Here at last are the records of the awful Holbrooke Quintet. I've felt for some time it was hopeless to expect Jack and/or Peers to remember to take them, and I think they should travel alright.

I hope you are all well and flourishing. I expect you know Jack conducted his *Sinfonietta* in Cheltenham (the L.P.O.) and then refused to do so in Hereford. The Cheltenham concert was a great success but an awful strain. He was in such a state of nerves I thought he might put his foot through a double-bass when he came on, and there was also some danger of his very moth-eaten dress clothes bursting!

104

In Hereford the L.S.O. didn't do too well with the *Sinfonietta*. I think they were annoyed at his refusal to function. The trouble was partly nerves but also the Three Choirs people had his name on the programme before they even asked him if he would function, and they had no seats for his people.

He was understandably annoyed!

> With very kind regards,
> Yours sincerely,
> Dick Jobson

(excerpt)

> The Laurels,
> December 1946

Dear Mr. Hill,

Thank you for your letter. I am very glad you think all is going well with Jack and Peers. I haven't seen much of them lately. At the same time I do know the difficulties. You see it is my privilege to be the confidant of both of them − and of Jack's brother Graham, and Mrs Moeran senior − so I have no doubts about the troubles. I am sure you are a great help to Jack, and I don't think I need to tell you that his mother is always happy to know he is with you. I expect she's told you that herself. It's a subject better discussed when we meet than written about. I am sure I can discuss it with you without disloyalty to Jack and Peers because I know you are good friends of theirs, and because I feel you are of the greatest help and value to Jack. You know he has a wide range of friends and not all of them help him in quite the best way.

For Heaven's sake don't remark to him that Elgar's Second Symphony was also in the key of E flat! I know that's been one of his excuses for shelving the work, and the *Sinfonietta* was supposed to break the sequence!

I sincerely hope we will see you this Summer.

> Yours
> Dick Jobson

(excerpt)

> The Laurels
> 6/1/47

Dear Mr. Hill,

Thank you very much for your letter and most excellent photo of Jack. I'm glad you thought him fit. I've been rather worried about him lately. I know the marriage is going badly, and that he is going on the razzle rather a lot and quite frankly when I saw him last I didn't think he was his old self at all. I'm afraid also it will affect his music. He will keep shying off the major works e.g. the E flat Symphony − and although I quite like the Oboe Quartet and think it a most pleasant work, I don't think it had the original Moeran fire. He is repeating himself too much. Oh dear – I do hope I'm being too pessimistic, but I feel very worried about Jack. I do hope we will see you soon. Please give my salutations to Mrs. Hill.

>   All the very best,
>   Dick Jobson

(excerpt)

>   The Laurels
>   11/10/49

Dear Mr. Hill,

Thank you very much for your card about your change of address.

Jack has vanished from my ken since June too. He stayed in the village for a few days and I am afraid was in a pretty bad way. He re-visited some of his old Kington associates with disastrous results. I feel very worried about him. He was terribly depressed at his inability to produce a worthy Symphony for the Hallé, but I got the strong impression that he was indeed going to pieces.

With all good wishes and please remember me to Mrs. Hill.

>   Yours in haste (as usual),
>   Dick Jobson

* * * * *

Between the above letters and the two which follow there occurred the sudden death of Jack. Further details of this tragic event will follow.

* * * * *

(excerpt)

>   The Laurels
>   8/1/52

Dear Mr. Hill,

Thank you very much for your card. I rather think I owe you this letter since last year. I do so wish you could get over here again. There is so much to tell you, and I should like you both to meet my wife.

Firstly re Jack. I was in Ireland in the Summer and visited Kenmare and his haunts there, also the Pier. I m afraid the good folk who knew and loved him so well there have little doubt about the matter.

I would be delighted to hear from you. Most of all I'd like to meet you both once more – there is much we could talk about.

With all good wishes,

>   Yours,
>   Dick Jobson

106

* * * * *

Over 20 years elapsed before I heard from Dick again. It was in December 1975 that I took part in a broadcast about Moeran on the Overseas Service of the BBC. I thought this might interest Dick, so I wrote to him in advance and received the following reply:

> The Laurels,
> December 2nd 1975
>
> Dear Mr. Hill,
>
> It was a most delightful surprise to get your letter this morning. Thank you very much for writing and for telling me of the broadcast. I will certainly try to hear it.
>
> I have never forgotten your visit here, and in fact a remark of Betty's has become a sort of family catchword – 'You see, my father plays the violin!' Please give her my regards, and congratulate her on an immortal understatement.
>
> Although I look in vain through the concert programmes in *The Telegraph* for Jack's name, I think he *is* beginning to be recognised.
>
> I did a bit of talking about Jack for Irish TV a year or two ago. They and I were hoping the BBC would show it in England, but nothing came of it. The team were a pleasant lot and played me a tape they had of Jack being interviewed by Eamon Andrews on which he said that pop music made him want to seek the nearest loo and vomit.
>
> I could wander on about 'E.J.' interminably, for much happened between your visit here and his death, and indeed since, which is not unrelated to our friendship. But one must eschew overdosing!
>
> I will take the liberty of adding a few personal details. Obviously my parents are dead. My mother died of cancer in 1950 and was nursed by someone whom I married. Although I married her before Jack's death they never met, a fact which makes me very sad. Pauline was born in Dublin and is very much in tune with Jack's Celtic spirit. I do wish they had met. We have no family.
>
> I have written enough for the present. It would be good to meet you and talk of Jack and of music. Once more please give my salutations to Betty.
>
> Yours very sincerely,
> Dick Jobson

What a lot had happened in the 30 years since we first met Dick and his family!

But more sorrow was to come, for when I wrote again in February 1978 I received an unexpected reply:

The Laurels
9/2/78

Dear Mr. Hill,

This morning your letter for Dick arrived, so I write straight away to say he died some time ago, to be precise a year and a month ago, on January 9th 1977. Quite suddenly, here one minute and then gone. But I was so glad to read your letter for he frequently talked of you, and I felt I was hearing from a friend. When J.M. died I had a great feeling of loss. I had never met Jack, but Dick was so enthusiastic about all those people he knew and liked, they became my unknown friends.

Yours,
Pauline Jobson

In addition to the shock and sadness of this letter from Dick's widow, came the realization that now I would never truly learn the cause of Jack's rapid decline in the last years. Dick's letter showed that he could have told us a lot, but personal contact with him had not been possible, owing to business and family commitments.

× * * * *

I received the following letters from Jack's mother, in one of which she states that Jack had lost the ability to compose:

The Rectory,
Ledbury
December 10th 1950

Dear Mr. Hill,

I am so grateful to both you and Mrs. Hill for your *real* sympathy, for I know what friends you were to Jack and how much he cared for you both, and therefore his passing means a great loss to you.

There have been so many rumours in the papers and incorrect statements, that I would like to tell you that our dear Jack died of cerebral haemorrhage. He was standing on the pier at Kenmare, when he was seen to fall, and a great gust of wind swept him into the river. A boat was at once put out and in a few minutes he was brought ashore; but nothing could be done. The report of the inquest was that he must have died instantaneously and painlessly before he reached the water. My other son went over to Ireland at once. Jack had been in Kenmare for seven months, living quietly there, and doing a little work. He loved the place and he was among friends.

They have laid him to rest in the little old churchyard of Kenmare. At present I don't seem able to realize that he has gone.

What a wonderful memorial he has left in his music! Again I do thank you both for your sympathy.

> Yours very sincerely,
> Esther Moeran

> The Rectory,
> Ledbury
> March 26th 1951

Dear Mr. Hill,

How very kind of you to send me the snaps of Jack! I do appreciate your thoughtfulness. It is a comfort to me to feel that there are others (like yourself) who really knew and loved him, and I am sure you know he valued the friendship of you and your wife.

Life goes on, but there is the terrible blank; like you, I cannot realize that Jack has really left us, and I find myself thinking 'I must write and tell Jack this', or, 'Jack would be so interested to know this', and then comes the realization – he's not there.

After months of silence I had a letter from him about two weeks before he passed away – which told me the great dread he had that his brain was growing weak. Of course this was really true, and I do not think he would ever have been able to write another big work, and that must have been a terrible trial to him, and it makes one so thankful to know that the end was so painless and peaceful. The rest of the letter was just full of his usual loving way of writing.

I am sending you the last photo we have of him, taken at Kenmare about two years ago. He looks very sad, but it is so like him as he often looked latterly; but when he left for Ireland, and I parted with him at the station, he looked smiling and happy, as he was really pleased to be going back to his old haunts. I had a few very cheerful letters, and then no more – except one wire to say he had been very ill, but was recovering. That was on the 1st May. I knew where he was latterly and that he was with friends who knew him well.

A number of his small possessions have been sent here, and I shall be so glad to send you something from his study that he used.

You must forgive this long letter, but when I begin to write about Jack, I think I do not know where to stop!

My kindest remembrances to Mrs. Hill.

> Yours very sincerely,
> Esther Moeran

The Rectory,
Ledbury
November 22nd 1951

Dear Mr. Hill,

I do not know if you have heard that there will be a memorial concert of Jack's chamber music on December 4th. I am sure you will like to go if possible, so I am sending you some tickets. If you are not able to use them please give them to a friend. I am not able to go, but my son Graham will be there. Peers is returning to Australia on December 19th.

With kind regards,
Esther Moeran

Betty and I went to this concert, which was well attended by an appreciative audience. The programme was:

R.B.A. GALLERIES.
Tuesday, December 8th, 1951.
at 8 p.m.
A MEMORIAL CONCERT
of the works of E. J. Moeran

String Quartet in A minor
Aeolian String Quartet

* * * * *

Sonata for Violoncello and Pianoforte
Peers Coetmore and Paul Hamburger

* * * * *

String Trio in G
London String Trio
Fantasy Quartet in one movement (1946)
(Dedicated to Leon Goossens)
Leon Goossens and the Carter String Trio

A criticism of the concert appeared in the Sunday *Observer*:

In London, at the R.B.A. Galleries, a memorial concert of works by the late E. J. Moeran was given, for which thirteen well-known instrumentalists gave their services, among them the composer's widow, the cellist Peers Coetmore. The music stood up far better to the test of a lengthy one-man programme than one would have expected, no doubt because, discursive as it is, it has a vigorous streak of rusticity which, as in Housman's poetry, strengthens rather than damages artistry, and there is a perfectly genuine musicality beneath its earthy, salty downrightness. Moeran had by no means finished his career when he died with such tragic suddenness.

Mrs Moeran's correspondence continued as follows:

The Rectory,
Ledbury
1952
Dear Mr. Hill,
At last I have finished looking over Jack's things and am sending you a little book-rest that he had always on the bookcase in his study at Kington, and I believe in his studio in London. Anyhow he always used it. I hope you will like it.

With kindest regards,
Yours sincerely,
Esther Moeran

The Rectory,
Ledbury
October 14th 1953
Dear Mr. Hill,
Thank you very much for your letter, which greatly interests me as I was under the impression that the uncompleted MSS of Jack's Second Symphony had either been lost or destroyed. Before he left me for Ireland for the last time I asked Jack about the Symphony and he told me he had finished two movements and was at work on the third, which did not satisfy him, and he should probably re-write it. He did not mention that he had left the MSS with Bax, or even shown it to him.

Jack appointed two executors in his will — my elder son Graham, and Sir Arnold Bax as literary executor. After Jack's death, Graham brought back with him from Ireland a bundle of MSS which were done up in a parcel, without examination, and sent to Sir Arnold Bax, who acknowledged their safe arrival, but neither Graham nor I received any subsequent report from him as to what the parcel contained, nor do I think that Jack's wife (who is now in Australia) was informed about them either. Before we take any action in the matter, I should be so grateful to you if you would let me know a little more in detail your authority for saying that Bax had in his possession the Symphony MSS. It would also be helpful both to my son and myself if you would advise us to whom they should be sent. We should be entirely happy, if this is not asking too much, for them to be sent to you, giving you a free hand to deal with them as you think best. If so, would you prefer to deal with the matter personally, or would you like me to ask my cousin Mr. Norman Hudson, a solicitor in London who has dealt with all the legal business in Jack's estate, to write to Bax's executors on our behalf? Do you happen to know who they are?

It would be a great thing if the MSS could be discovered. Please let me know what you think.

> With kind regards,
> Yours very sincerely,
> Esther Moeran

The silver-mounted bookrest so kindly sent by his mother, together with some scores and books from Jack himself, will ever remain my most treasured possessions. Further correspondence with Mrs Moeran ceased with her death, shortly after her last letter to me.

The next letter, dealing with the saga of the missing manuscripts, came from Julian Herbage, instigator of the BBC 'Music Magazine' programme which, with Anna Instone, he ran for 20 years:

> 52 Basildon Court,
> Devonshire Street,
> London W.1
> 2nd March 1954

Dear Mr. Hill,

The Rev. Graham Moeran suggested that you might be interested in the following matter.

I was recently asked to look through the music manuscripts left by the late Sir Arnold Bax. Actually there was nothing important by Bax himself, but I came across a number of MSS which I was certain were the work of E. J. Moeran. I at once got in touch with his brother, who confirmed that he had brought some MSS from Ireland when he went over for Jack's funeral, and that he had given those to Bax, who was Jack's 'literary' executor.

It has taken me a little while to get these MSS delivered from the solicitor's office where I first examined them, but I have them now in my flat, and have sorted them into rough order.

The two most important works appear to be sketches in short score of (a) an Overture, and (b) a Symphonic movement, of which the first page is dated '11/2/48'. There is also part of a movement scored for a String Quartet, some Part Songs, including a setting of the folksong 'It was happy and delightful', several songs, the words only (with space for the tunes) of what was evidently intended to be a collection of Ballads, a short score of the Rondo from the Violin Concerto, the full score of a Fanfare for Red Army Day 1944, and several other odds and ends, including several pages of sketches, some of them I think relating to the Symphonic Movement.

112

So far I have done little more than get the papers in some order — they were in utter confusion when I got them and it will be some time before I will have an opportunity to go through them more thoroughly, as I am extremely busy at the moment building the programmes of the Promenade Concerts.

Please let me know if you are interested in all this. I don't think I have ever had the pleasure of meeting you, though Jack, of course, was an old friend of mine.

> Yours very truly,
> Julian Herbage

I shall always regret that I was unable to take advantage of the kind offer by Jack's mother that I should receive all the music that his brother Graham brought back from Ireland. Unfortunately I was deeply involved with business worries at this time, and felt that I could not take on further responsibilities. So I had reluctantly to refuse this proposal, and also that of Mr Herbage.

I could not have foreseen that these precious MSS would become scattered, lost for a while, and eventually turn up in Autralia.

How I wish that I could have acted in this matter when the opportunity was offered!

* * * * *

The final letter I will quote from came recently from Pauline Jobson, in reply to some queries I had put to her regarding the last nine months of Jack's life:

> The Laurels,
> New Radnor
> 20/4/80

Dear Mr. Hill,

I cannot give you absolute information about Jack living in Kenmare from January 1950 until he died, but I think he did. I should remember, for Dick and I went to Kenmare after Jack had died, and stayed in the hotel he lived in. Hotel is a grandiose name for a dark, damp, depressing house with a tall lady in complete black, walking around with a chatelaine clanking as she moved. I imagine, even in its heyday during Edward's reign, guests could not be impressed by linoleum-covered floors rather than carpets. I was younger then and impatient to move to comfort and edible food. Now I realize how stupid I was. A person I do remember meeting there was a dentist, who spoke in glowing terms of Jack. 'Ah, a gentleman, a fine gentleman he was.'

113

Later Dick told me that he and Jack had gone to this dentist's brother's funeral, to look for local colour and custom. Later, when I wanted new false teeth the dentist supplied them free of charge, he was so touched that Jack should have shown respect for the dead man by attending the funeral.

There was some sort of Folly near this hotel where Jack used to play the piano and compose. We saw it from a distance, the lady in black objected to us going there, and as she held sway in the household, and the key was on her chatelaine, we were not allowed to view.

No-one mentioned the word suicide.

As regards Jack's addiction, Dick knew of it quite wll, for he came here at times to recover when he had been on a very bad binge. Once Dick was surprised to meet him in the village street. Jack had come to New Radnor, heard Dick's mother was not well, so he booked into the pub as (to quote as I remember it) 'I am not fit company for a lady in my present condition'). Graham his brother spent a great deal of time and endless trouble to conceal from their mother this weakness. We were never certain if she found out. Peers swore she knew nothing about this drinking habit before their marriage. Pat Ryan (clarinet, Hallé) said she must have known; all the musical world knew, and Peers moved with these people. But she was quite determined to marry Jack to promote her position as a musician.

As regards the break-up of the marriage, again I can only remember what Dick told me. One thing was, the night before the wedding Jack told Dick, who was Best Man, 'This marriage is a disaster.' Dick asked 'Why go on with it?' 'I have given her my word as a gentleman. I cannot break my word,' was Jack's reply.

Like you, Dick quite enjoyed Peers as a person, and I was sorry to miss her when she paid a visit to this country, about a year before she died. I was away, she telephoned from Bath or somewhere, came, and Dick entertained her at the pub, and quite enjoyed his evening.

Dick and Pat Ryan talked a lot about Jack − his drinking, the fact that Peers was disastrous for him, pressure put to bear on him to finish something for the Cheltenham Festival, his great love for Norfolk, the critics writing about his work − which brought the remark from Jack, 'Never knew I was so clever, Dick.'

My kindest regards to you both,
Pauline Jobson

I think the preceding letters give some indication of Jack's latter days and death.

When we first knew him he was at the height of his powers: the Violin Concerto, the *Sinfonietta*, and the Cello Concerto all belong to this period.

114

Then came the ill-fated marriage, which he undertook partially to please his mother, who was anxious to find someone to steady him and look after him – and who shall blame her? Jack's father was very fond of Peers. We also liked her, and so did Dick Jobson, but we soon saw that she was not the wife for Jack. She had already had one unsuccessful marriage, and was to re-marry twice more after Jack's death.

The real problem was alcohol, which made him unstable. It was not a constant craving; in fact he could abstain for lengthy periods – then the balloon would burst and he indulged himself to the full. I had seen him in the latter state once or twice, but never was he obstreperous or difficult to handle – quite the reverse. He would become excessively polite and reserved, gradually sinking into a benign stupor.

Jack was badly wounded in the First World War, a piece of shrapnel becoming lodged too near the brain for removal by surgery. In view of the Coroner's verdict it seems likely that this war-wound caused Jack's death and his fall into the River Kenmare. No water was found in his lungs.

As Jack stated in his last postcard, dated 24th February 1950, he had found 'A lovely place to live in County Wicklow, 17 miles from Dublin'. It has recently come to light that this place was Delgany, and that he was happy in himself and with his work.

This brief state of affairs came to an end towards the end of March, when he visited an occulist in Dublin, who sent him to a specialist; a pressure on the brain or severe heart trouble was diagnosed.

Jack told no-one of his troubles, except possibly his mother, but began to drink heavily again.

He returned to Kenmare in June and remained there until his death in December. During that last six months he led a sober and secluded life, but was quite unable to compose.

One can only feel sympathy for Jack, who, though blamed by some for his recourse to alcohol, nevertheless had to live with the ever-present knowledge of a hidden danger to his brain. Much should be understood and forgiven.

* * * * *

INQUEST TRIBUTES

At the inquest, Dr W O'Sullivan, Coroner for South Kerry, who sat with a jury at the Courthouse, Kenmare, returned a verdict that Mr. Moeran 'came by his death from natural causes, namely cerebral haemorrhage, and fell into the water at Kenmare Pier on December 1st.'

Dr D P O'Callaghan, M.O. H. Kilgarvan, said he was present as the body was brought ashore, and on examination found life extinct. After a post-mortem examination medical opinion was that there was no water in the lungs, and that Mr. Moeran was dead before entering the water.

The Coroner, in extending sympathy to the wife, mother and brother of Mr. Moeran, observed that he was a cultured gentleman who was held high in the world of music and was in the top flight of musical composers.

Dr O'Callaghan, in associating himself with the expression of sympathy, commented that the composer was a man of great charm and had endeared himself to all. He had a great love for Ireland, particularly for Kenmare and its inhabitants, and had repeatedly said that it was from Kenmare seashore he got his inspiration.

Mr Thomas Palmer, Old Bridge Street, Kenmare, a farmer, said he was cycling to his farm near the pier around 4 p.m. on December 1st and saw Mr Moeran walking down the pier towards the end. He saw him looking into the water there and next saw him disappear. He went down to the end of the pier and saw him floating away. He reported the matter and helped to recover the body.

Mr John O'Brien, an employee of Kerry Co. Council, said he visited Mr Moeran at the Lansdown annexe at lunch time and Mr Moeran made an appointment to meet him there again at 6 p.m.

The funeral took place on Monday. The Rector of Kenmare (Canon Armstrong) conducted the service and the lesson was read by Prebendary W G Moeran. The interment followed in the old churchyard, Kenmare.

* * * * *

How amused Jack would have been to read the quaint language in his own obituary notice — especially to be called 'a cultured gentleman'! Did the reporter but know, he had penetrated to the heart of Jack's sense of humour — the reader may recall how he loved to look for queer inscriptions on tombstones, and how he read these aloud to us in Kington churchyard in 1945, and I recall his delight over such famous organists' names as Alcock, Peasegood, Thalben Ball, etc.

Our grandson Robert is a great admirer of Moeran's music, and has recently visited Kenmare, which he reached by a long walk over the glorious Kerry landscape. He was able to talk with some of the country folk who still remember Jack, and he came away with the lasting impression that he was held in deep love and affection by the people of Kenmare, even to this day. 'He has already become Kenmare's legend, a hero in fact,' he was told.

Apparently Jack was almost penniless towards the end, but luckily he had a good friend in the landlord of the hotel, who put him up, free of charge, in a lodge which he owned.

On the day of the funeral the whole town turned out to provide a moving farewell.

Robert visited the old churchyard. He said, 'It is now very overgrown and I didn't hold much hope of finding any sign of Moeran's grave. But I literally stumbled over it at one end of the churchyard overlooking the river. It is a small, neat stone at the head of a stone bed, now overgrown. On it is this inscription:

> To the memory of Ernest John Moeran
> the composer who died 1st December
> 1950, aged 55. He died in the mountain
> country which he loved so well.

Robert explored the town and countryside and, in his own words, 'It soon became apparent why Jack did not want to leave Kenmare, and so perhaps it was the best thing that he should die there, among a race of people who all loved him and understood him.'

* * * * *

In retrospect it seems poetically right that Jack should have met his death in 'Some lonely waters'. This beautiful work was the cause of our friendship, and somehow his end was foreshadowed in its dying cadence. Of all his output this is the one work which I can only occasionally bear to hear.

* * * * *

No one could presume to place Moeran among the great composers. There are over-wise critics who delight in finding passages in his music which they claim to be influenced by so-and-so composer. This may

117

be the case, but all British composers of his generation took a look at current trends, especially those in Europe. There is to be found Brahms in Elgar; Stravinsky, Prokokiev and Elgar in Walton; Jazz and Delius in Lambert, etc. Jack Moeran would have been the last to claim a unique originality of expression, and I am sure that such notions did not bother him.

What did concern him deeply was to express his vision in the most perfect manner − and with very few exceptions he was able to achieve this.

He was not an innovator, and listened intently to other composer's works, old and new, being content to absorb what appealed to him. His innate musicality was the dominant factor, for when genius drives the pen, questions of plagiarism do not hold a place of much importance.

Never was a composer's music so expressive of the man himself, and therein lies its fascination, for the mixture of Irish and English cultures was bound to produce an unusual and exciting flavour.

In spite of Jack having been brought up in the atmosphere of an Anglican vicarage, he was not religious in an orthodox sense. He never discussed such matters with me, nor did he go to church − except to get married!

He was in many ways a very private man, though he enjoyed convivial company when in the mood. It is interesting that in several photos showing Jack alongside such friends as Warlock, Van Dieran and Lambert, he is always standing apart, self-contained and slightly aloof.

Except for Warlock, whose tragic death left a lasting scar, it was Arnold Bax to whom Jack felt most akin. Both were deeply moved by the Celtic spirit, and Jack often stayed with him. Bax was also a shy, reserved character and I recall Jack telling me that when the former was asked to become Master of the King's Music, Jack was staying with him at the time. Bax said he couldn't face such onerous publicity, but Jack persuaded him to accept the honour.

Moeran's music, however, shows little obvious debt to Bax, which is remarkable in view of his admiration for the latter's *Tintagel, The Garden of Fand* and the Violin Concerto. There is a kindred spirit, however.

Jack's two concertos are my own favourites among his works, though the *Sinfonietta* is, perhaps, the most perfect − a masterpiece, as he used to call some of Delius. The G minor Symphony is a considerable achievement but is more derivative than the two concertos, the later one for cello showing much originality, and perfectly expresses all that Jack had been trying to say throughout his life.

This music will not appeal to those who seek profundity, in the cerebral sense, or technical bravura; but the listener attuned to its intense lyricism will come to love it beyond price.

It may appear that Delius occurs too often in this story, but this composer was not only responsible for me getting to know Jack, but was also a lasting bond between us to the end.

Before closing this tale of our friendship with Jack, I would like to quote the moving obituary by Sir Arnold Bax, who knew him well for 30 years, and whose telling phrases express what I have tried to convey throughout this book:

> It must have been in the summer of 1919 that I was invited to an evening party somewhere in Kensington. This was my first encounter with Jack Moeran and the beginning of a close friendship which was to continue unbroken until the tragic day when his body was found in the Kenmare river.
>
> At the time of our earliest acquaintance he was about to be demobilized after serving in the army all through the war and, in the course of it, suffering a head wound to the after-effects of which may perhaps be attributed a certain instability in his character later on.
>
> He told me that he was a pupil of John Ireland, whom he always declared to be a most painstaking and conscientious teacher. Ireland himself reciprocated Moeran's respect and thought very highly of the latter's gifts as a composer. He had every right to be proud of his pupil.
>
> Jack's predilection for the Irish (or rather Kerry) scene must have been wholly instinctive and emotional. He knew nothing of Irish history, nothing of the heroic legends, nothing of the Celtic literary revival. Very wisely he refused to take part in any discussion of Irish politics, even if he was aware that such matters for violent debate existed.
>
> But he knew and loved the Kerry people and understood unerringly how to get on with them. His friendly and unpretentiously straightforward manner was precisely the same whether he was in the company of a brewery peer, an hotel boots, a priest, an out-at-elbow tramp, or even a drink-sodden and bellicose tinker at Puck Fair in Killorglin.
>
> The people of Kenmare adored him. One of them remarked to me, 'If ever there was a move to elect a mayor of this town, Jack Moeran would be everyone's first choice.' His popularity was immense, even, it must be admitted, sometimes to the point of embarrassment.

Everyone who knew Jack liked him, for he could have had no enemy. Kenmare must have been mourning him, and if the ancient keen were still to be heard in Kerry, as it was when I was young, it would surely have been wailed over the dead body of the village's old friend.

His was a simple soul, and a lovable one. 'Ave atque vale!'

Appendix 'A'

An article in *The Gramophone*, March 1947,
written by Robin Lea (Lionel Hill)

E J Moeran – an appreciation

When the British Council decided to inaugurate their fine series of gramophone recordings of British music with the issue of E. J. Moeran's Symphony in G minor, there can be little doubt that this composer's name was unknown to the majority of music lovers.

Such a state of affairs is not surprising, seeing that prior to the first performance of this Symphony in 1938, Moeran's published output was mainly devoted to chamber music and works for small orchestra, and was not, therefore, of a type upon which to build a reputation in this country. Within the last ten years, however, Moeran has shown a remarkable prodigality, and has given the world two fine concertos, a *Sinfonietta*, a *Rhapsody* for piano and orchestra, an Overture, an Oboe Quartet, and several songs.

It would appear, therefore, that Moeran is tending towards an assured position as a first-rank symphonic composer, and worthy of greater attention than he is afforded in musical performances and literary appreciation.

He was born at Isleworth on December 31st, 1894, his mother being an East Anglian from Norfolk, and his father an Irishman and a priest of the Protestant Church. Up to the age of fourteen, Moeran had little chance of hearing music; but upon going to Uppingham School he was able for the first time to hear real music, and also came under the kindly, but understanding, guidance of Sterndale Bennett, who was then head music-master at this school.

Leaving Uppingham, Moeran entered The Royal College of Music, and studied under that fine teacher C. V. Stanford. A period of active service with the Colours during World War One lasted until he was discharged in 1919, after which Moeran resumed his long interrupted studies, this time with John Ireland, to whom he owes, in part, something of the mastery of technique and form which is manifest in his works.

Moeran's first published composition appeared in 1921, and consisted of a set of piano pieces which were soon followed by a further set, together with a brilliant *Toccata* for piano. This latter piece, which is extremely exhilarating but difficult to play, has recently been included in the Royal Academy's list of examination pieces for top-grade pupils.

By 1925 had appeared two orchestral rhapsodies, a very fine string quartet, a sonata for violin and piano, and songs.

During the 'thirties, Moeran was steadily working on his Symphony, but found time to write some exquisite smaller-scale works. Among the latter are two pieces for small orchestra, *Whythorne's Shadow* and *Lonely Waters*, both of which show Moeran's lyrical and contemplative vein to perfection.

Another beautifully expressive work written at this period is *Nocturne*, for baritone, chorus and orchestra. This is a setting to words by Robert Nichols, and is dedicated to the memory of Frederick Delius. It is a work full of poignant beauty, and is long overdue for more frequent performance.

No article on Moeran would be complete without reference to his fine folk-song researches, especially in regard to his beloved Norfolk. He has collected 150 local songs which had not been previously noted down, and his activities in this field are well-known in folk-music circles.

It is not surprising, therefore, that Moeran writes vocal music with a rare understanding of the human voice. Two fine examples of his part-song writing are *Songs of Springtime* and *Phyllida and Corydon*, which are given occasionally over the wireless, and are well worth an effort to hear.

The Symphony was eventually completed in 1937, and has since brought world-wide recognition to its creator. It is a brilliantly-orchestrated document of great emotional power, revealing Moeran to be a master of lyrical drama, and is, perhaps, the equal of the symphonies of Elgar, Vaughan Williams and Walton.

For some years past Moeran has been wont to spend a considerable part of each year in Eire, and it is in the Violin Concerto that is expressed his affection for the lovely County Kerry. The whole work is permeated by a nostalgic, almost heartbreaking beauty, which is only temporarily relieved in the very lively second movement. In the hands of a violinist of the temperament and technique adequate to the work, this Concerto is capable of holding its place among the few really great compositions in this form.

Moeran is an inveterate country-lover, and passionately desires the remote atmosphere of certain parts of these islands for the true expression of his musical genius. When, therefore, he went to live in the wild Welsh border country during the late war, it is not surprising that an extremely productive period followed, among the results of which must be mentioned a fine *Sinfonietta* and a very original Cello Concerto of much beauty. Both these works are most imaginatively scored, and reveal Moeran at the height of his powers. One finds here the quintessence of all that had gone before, expressed with a sure economy of means and a wealth of finely-wrought lyricism.

In retrospect one feels that Moeran has never looked back. He has always written slowly, and his output is not as prolific as that of some of his contemporaries; but he has not made the cardinal mistake of repeating himself, and each new composition has shown a new facet of an original mind.

One might, perhaps, sum up by expressing the view that Moeran is one of the very few modern composers who can successfully employ twentieth-century technique to express an essentially poetic personality. The emotional content of this music never falters or becomes tiresome, but is a happy amalgam of boisterous melody and deep-felt soliloquy.

At the age of fifty-two, the graphic curve of Moeran's achievement shows a steady upward trend, and there would appear to be no reason why his ultimate position in British music should not be among this country's greatest composers.

It is to be hoped that the recording companies have noted the growing demand from readers of this paper for an early issue of Moeran's Violin Concerto. A considerable body of informed musical opinion has realised for some time past that this concerto not only has few equals in music of our time, but possesses qualities which place it among the finest creations of this century.

It is of vital importance, therefore, that attention be drawn in the proper quarter to the rare opportunity which now exists to place this beautiful work on record for posterity.

We have in this country two musicians who hold the highest opinion of the work in question. John Barbirolli has made no secret of his desire to record this Concerto, if possible with that fine violinist Albert Sammons.

Unfortunately for British music, Mr. Sammons has decided to give up concerto playing in public, and to devote his great talent to teaching. But such is his love for the Moeran Concerto, and the high regard he entertains for Barbirolli, that an understanding exists between these eminent musicians to devote their energies to the making of an authentic recording, should an opportunity arise *within the near future*.

It can be appreciated that time is short. A great but fleeting opportunity lies within reach of the recording companies to effect the perfect realisation of a British masterpiece. The Walton Violin Concerto was allowed to stray into a foreign recording studio, with dire results.

A similar fate must not befall the Moeran Concerto.

Appendix 'B'

The Moeran correspondence

The following extracts are taken from the many air-mail letters that Jack Moeran wrote to Peers Coetmoor, mostly while she was on tours for ENSA in the Middle East, Australia and New Zealand. It is an interesting co-incidence that these letters exactly cover the period of my friendship with the composer.

Explanatory comments are enclosed within square brackets.

Peers' letters to Jack appear to have been destroyed, as there is no trace of them.

1943

October (undated). Destination unstated. From Shelbourne Hotel, Dublin
… Now, please write and tell me you would like me to write a concerto specially for you, and I give you my promise that I will put my whole heart into it.

Moreover, it won't be like the last work, which was dedicated to Harriet Cohen and which to my certain knowledge contains more than its fair share of tripe. [*Rhapsody* for piano and orchestra, a work I hold in much higher regard than he seems to have done!] I had to do it in order to carry out an old promise, also because of my friendship (of many years' standing) with Arnold Bax.

But in the case of this proposed Cello Concerto, it would be quite different because I would be wanting to write it for you, genuinely, and for nobody else.

If you don't want a Concerto from me, please be brutal if you like and don't hesitate to say so, but you did in an airy kind of way say, 'When are you going to write me a concerto?'

I assure you that once I get down to writing you a work you will get nothing other than scrappy notes from me otherwise!

Jack,

P.S. If you consent to take a Concerto from me on trust, I am afraid that the idea of a Sonata or Sonatina for cello and piano must go West.

I hope you will agree, i.e. to the Concerto idea, because I somehow conceive you and your playing in terms of cello and orchestra.

Actually, I did begin to think of something of this nature on the boat yesterday, so *please* write and tell me you would like me to go on with it.

I think I can give you my word that if you want me to write a Cello Concerto especially for you, I will be able to go one better than I did in the Violin Concerto; only give me the O.K. or your blessing on the project, and then I think I will be able to walk the Kerry mountains with a real happy objective in view.

October 10th   Shelbourne Hotel. Dublin

My dear Peers,

I had a wonderfully peaceful and beautiful crossing yesterday, ending up with a perfect sunset over the Wicklow Mountains as we approached the Irish coast.

I have been practising my songs all the afternoon with the singer, Violet Burne, who is going to do them on Friday. We have decided to do only two of the new ones this time, one a James Joyce setting, and the other a Seumas O'Sullivan poem. As soon as I shall have had a day or two at a piano there will be a whole cycle of the latter gentleman's verse, but so far, of the four I have done, it seems more feasable to do the one separate one, *Invitation in Autumn*, and to leave the rest for subsequent recitals.

There are two more poems I want to set, and actually I have got the music of them in my head, so it will be mainly a matter of committing it to paper. [Refer to pages 37 and 38 in main text. The original O'Sullivan set comprised seven songs, but only six were published — *Evening, The Poplars, A Cottager, The Dustman, Lullaby, The Herdsman*. The cycle is dedicated to Violet Burne, while *Invitation in Autumn* is dedicated to Parry Jones.]

What is really more concerning my mind is to write something for you ... your 'cello playing seems to have got into my system to such an extent that I can only think in terms of yourself and your instrument.

Anyway, my dear Peers, do let me try and show my appreciation of you by writing a really nice work for you.

I think that when the time comes for it to be finished it would be so splendid if you were to play the first performance of it. I know that my position, such as it is, is sufficiently strong with either the B.B.C. or the Royal Philharmonic for me to insist on that, once the work is finished.

Please write soon, because once I get down next Saturday to my beloved Kerry, I want to be in a position to know whether to go ahead. You remember I told you I think of my themes when I walk the mountains there, and if I thought you were going to back me up I really think the time is just about right for me to rise again to concerto form.

I think, Peers, that if you really agree to my piece ... that Nature might be kind, and that with luck I might think of something which might be more worthwhile than anything I have managed to turn out so far.

[Rest of letter missing.]

15th October   Telegram from Dublin to Peers at 55 Belsize Lane. N.W.3

Have started 'Cello Concerto. Hope you don't mind. Writing. Jack Moeran.

20th October   Kenmare
My dear Peers,
In my letter of yesterday I advised you to make the tour of the East, but in view of what I received from you in your letter which came today, I am afraid my baser and more selfish nature came to the surface and I wired to you not to go.

If you will trust me to try and work for you with this Concerto you can cut engagements for a time and come down to Kington. We could walk together on Hergest Ridge and Bradnor and work out tunes. But I am bound to say that they will be Kerry inspired ones − I hope you won't mind! I have started thinking out themes for you, and I must go on before I leave my beloved Kerry.

I am going for a walk to see the sun to the West over our lovely bay. I shall have paper and pencil with me and I may jot down something for our work together.

October 22nd   Postcard from Kenmare
I intend running over to Valencia Island on Tuesday for a couple of nights. I think I am really thinking out something for the Concerto.
    J.M.

October 26th   O'Connell's Hotel. Caherciveen. Co. Kerry
My dear Peers,
I hope you won't think me strange and sentimental (à la German Classics), but I thought of a tune in bed last night just after I had put out the light, which I thought then, and still do on more mature reflection the morning after, will fill the bill as the second subject of the first movement. I hope you don't mind sonata form, in spite of the dicta of our Sibelians, but I was so imbued with it for many years that I find it natural to think that way.

I feel rather homesick tonight for my old island of Valencia, where I wrote so much of my Symphony and [Violin] Concerto. God knows when I'll see you again (we are three miles here from the coast.)
    Your loving Jack.
[Peers was about to go on an ENSA tour of the Middle East.]

October 31st   Kenmare
My dear Peers,
You noble and generous letter came last night, so I sent you a wire that you may know I will come back to see a bit of you before you go away. If I know that I have your affection I can go on with the 'Cello Concerto at Kington just as if I were here.

November 16th   Kington

I am most colossally hard at work at the moment. I am on a somewhat elaborate and exceedingly free arrangement for 'cello and piano of the Irish tune 'Johnny Asthore' etc. This one – *

It should be ready and copied out for you when I come on Thursday, also some more, I hope. It will be six long months before I shall have the chance of doing any work with you again.

December 15th   Kington. Airmail to Special concerts. 55515 A.P.O

My dearest Peers,

I felt absolutely miserable in London after you had gone, especially in the Belsize Park area with you no longer there. At Kington I can go into the pastures or up the hill and somehow feel that you are there with me in a telepathic way. Don't forget to think of me up on Bradnor Hill planning out my music.

    All my devoted and fondest love,
        Jack.

December 27th   Airmail letter to Cairo

I go on missing you more than ever. I suppose I must go to London in about a month's time to make my American broadcast records. [With his usual reticence he made no reference to the author about this broadcast.] I expect I shall stay with the Hills at Seer Green.**

    Goodbye for the present, my dear lovely Peers,
        from your own Jack.

December 30th   Kington. Airmail letter to Cairo

My dearest Peers,

I am starting this late at night. I have been at work yesterday and today and added another song to my Seumas O'Sullivan set. That makes five now: I think there will have to be two more, but I shan't do them yet awhile. The one I have done today is strange: it is called *The Herdsman*, and is about slow moving cattle. As the vocal part is very largely on one note, it is possible that it will not find favour

---

  * A folk-song used by Jack in *Irish Love Song*, for piano, 1926.
  ** See p. 30 in main text for this visit.

128

easily with our brilliantly intelligent English singers. I think these are my swan song so far as solo songs are concerned.*

Singers are so stupid and uninterested in music it seems more worthwhile to conserve one's energies for writing music in other forms.

The pity of it is in my case that I think I am better at songs than at anything else, ie, some of my songs are my very best works.

I think of you so much and with all my love, and I always shall.

Jack.

1944

January 2nd   Kington. Airmail letter to Cairo

My dearest Peers,

I have just listened in to a chamber concert. The Hirsch Quartet played Haydn Op. 73 in G minor and Kodaly in D. The former was new to me and I liked it very much. No doubt you know it backwards. I was disappointed in the Kodaly: there are plenty of good things in it, but I found it terribly disjointed and far too orchestral in effect. Double-stopping seemed to abound by the sound of things, and I must say that I find a 'vertical' quartet which is almost devoid of polyphony, as this one is, or sounded to me, very wearisome to listen to for three movements on end.

Now I am going via the post office and on up the hills, probably by Hergest and the wood.

All my undying love, darling Peers,

Jack.

January 4th   Kington. Airmail letter to Cairo

My darling Peers,

It is now three weeks since you went away, and I am still awaiting news of your safety. It is a mockery trying to compose this snappy Overture for E.N.S.A. in my present state of anxiousness. [*Overture for a Masque*] However, I am forcing myself to do it somehow so far.

All my fondest and undying love, my darling,

Jack.

January 5th   Kington. Airmail letter to Cairo

My own darling,

This is indeed a red-letter day. I got your cable this morning. Peers, my dearest, I do feel so relieved and quite a different being.

Now, my work will go ahead like a house on fire. Today I have actually

---

* Not so. More folk-songs were to follow; also James Joyce's *Rahoon*.

approached my E.N.S.A. Overture with zest and the idea that I am going to make it really snappy and exciting for the troops to listen to.

Your loving Jack.

January 7th Kington.Airmail letter to Cairo

My darling Peers,

What a difference that news of you has made to my everyday life. Now I am able to apply myself to my Overture, with real enthusiasm for work. It is getting on slowly at the moment. I am just on an awkward bit and once I am over that I expect to go ahead pretty fast. But I am longing to finish it and then to get at the 'cello sonata.

I shall go and seek what thematic inspiration for that work will come to me in the Spring where I walked with you in Bucks.

Lionel Hill (Seer Green) sent me a miniature score of Delius' *Appalachia* for a Christmas present and my Mother has given me the records of it for my Birthday.

My dentist has lent me records of Tchaikovsky's Second Symphony, the 'Little Russian'. It is a model of orchestration and old Tchaik, when he does go all-Russian I'm thinking of you with ever-increasing love, seems to do so to more effect than some of the Nationalist composers.

Yours own Jack.

January 12th Kington. Airmail letter to Cairo

My darling Peers,

I met the organist of Leominster Priory church who made such a hash of turning over for me when we played the Delius 'Cello Sonata. I now find that the unfortunate man is a stutterer. This is interesting to me, because years ago when I once played at a Thursday music meeting of the old Oxford and Cambridge musical club a member turned over for me in a Mozart piano Sonata. Fortunately, I knew the piece by heart, as he, too, was a man with a terrible speech impediment and stuttered badly. Do the two go together? I imagine they both, although both could read music well, became in a mental state of dither at the moment of action in turning over and that their joints and muscles refused to function in synchronization with the brain. In other words, they stuttered in turning over pages. That might be an interesting poser for a psycho-therapist.

I am full of energy as regards keeping at work but, honestly, I wish the Overture were finished with and I were on to something else. It is a commissioned work, as you know, and is not my top notch; the fact is I am doing it as a duty engendered by the War, and working to a time-table I am not able to follow my normal method of extreme self-criticism. [He is referring here to the *Overture for a Masque*.]

Ever your own loving Jack.

January 20th   Kington. Airmail to ENSA, Middle East Forces
My darling Peers,
I am longing to be writing a big work for you, but I am now getting on quite fast
with Walter Legge's Overture, so soon I shall be working on something for you.
        My love always and for ever. Jack.

January 26th   Kington. Airmail to M.E.F. Cairo
My darling Peers,
My Overture has made a spurt this last two days, so much so that I hope to finish
the composition of it comfortably before I go to Glasgow next week. Then I shall
take it to London for the parts to be copied. It remains to be seen whether Boosey
and Hawkes will succeed in doing this in time for me to hand over the material
to E.N.S.A. by the last day of February.
        I am going for today's walk now, 3.30 p.m. and shall cut afternoon tea. We
are having the evening meal early as there is a B.B.C. Symphony concert tonight
with a good programme including the Delius Violin Concerto with Albert
Sammons.
        Now that the Overture is so nearly finished, when I go for my walk today I
am going to let myself go in my thoughts of music for you, my darling, for the
'cello Sonata which I am going to do first before the Concerto.
        I believe the Overture is going to sound decidedly exciting.

February 8th   Kington. Airmail to ENSA, 27 General Hospital, MEF
My darling Peers,
I have been having somewhat of a job with my *Fanfare for Red Army Day*.
The Ministry kept ringing me up at Glasgow telling me different each time as to
the instrumentation required. Finally, since I got back here I have contacted Flash
Harry [Sir Malcolm Sargent] on the telephone and got down to final brass tacks,
so I am writing it for three large brass bands, two of which will be on the stage
and one in the auditorium.

February 12th   Kington. Airmail letter to ENSA, MEF
My darling Peers,
My records of *Appalachia* have come this week, but I have been so desperately busy
with the Red Army Fanfare and Legge's Overture that I have had only time to try
it over once. The Fanfare has no accidentals in it at all, being diatonic throughout...
        Tomorrow is Assize Sunday at Hereford and my *Te Deum* is to be sung in
the cathedral ... As for the Overture, now that it is getting into full score it is
turning out really well and I believe and hope you will like it when eventually
you hear it. ... I am beginning to work out the shape of the 'cello sonata, though
I can't get to it exclusively till Legge's score is polished off.

February 17th   Kington. Airmail letter to ENSA, MEF
My darling Peers,
... My Overture is finished and scored and I am now making the fair copy ...
On Wednesday I shall go to the Albert Hall proceedings and hear my row for
the massed bands, i.e. provided they give me a ticket. Michael Mulliner ... came
to my rescue last week by lending me a handbook on military band instrumentation
when I was hard put to it to know how to set about my Fanfare.

Undated   Kington. Airmail letter to ENSA, MEF
My darling Peers,
... I think it [The Overture] turns out to be quite a good little work, what you
might call athletic in style. Consequently it has reams of long string passages in
semiquavers, and the consequence is that it takes the devil of a time to write out.

February 21st   In the train near Hereford. Airmail to ENSA, MEF
My darling Peers,
... The B.B.C. are putting on some Elgar performances this week in commemora-
tion of his death. Last night the First Symphony was magnificently played under
Henry Wood. Tomorrow evening Boult does the Second Symphony: I may not
hear this, as the Hills have only an indifferent radio set. An E.M.G. hand-made
gramophone and a splendid library of records is their strong suit.

April 13th   Kenmare. Airmail letter to 84 Base, Middle East
Darling Peers,
... I have given up the Sonata idea, and I am in the thick of your Concerto ...
        Your own Jack.

April 15th   Kenmare. Airmail letter to 84 Base, Middle East
My darling Peers,
... meanwhile I am attempting to pick-up the inspiration for our own 'cello
concerto in Kerry. Darling, beloved Peers, I am trying to work for you; you as
an artist and as my dear love are all that matters.
        Jack.

May 3rd   Victoria Hotel. Cork. Airmail to ENSA, MEF
My darling,
... In the afternoon I was examining the compositions for the Feis, and came upon
a masterpiece of a song among some awful rubbish. Finally, I went to a really
good performance of *Madam Butterfly* at the Opera House ... I have always had
a weakness for Puccini.
        Your own Jack.

132

May 8th   Gresham Hotel. Dublin. Airmail to ENSA, MEF
My darling,
It is alright about our Concerto! You will be asked to give the first performance here in the Capital Theatre with a repeat performance from the studio. Also, we shall be able to have as many rehearsals as we want, even eight or ten! I have fixed all this with Radio Eirann authorities. Meanwhile, I have been working out the thematic and harmonic scheme of the work, and what I long for is for you to come back to me. You will have to give me some technical help over the 'cello part.
      Jack.

July 11th   Kington. Airmail to ENSA, MEF
My darling Peers,
... As for myself, since I came back here and in my quiet home with Mamma and Aunt Winnie (great company, she is) I am quite content. I have in fact just finished a work, a song-cycle to Irish poems.

July 24th   Kington, Airmail to ENSA, MEF
My darling,
Since writing to you last, I have played over the Piatigorsky records of the Schumann Concerto; they are really excellent ... I am not as a rule a Schumann addict, but I like this work.

August 10th   Kington. Airmail to ENSA, MEF
Darling Peers,
... You evidently understood the neccessity for following to a certain extent where fancy happens to lead, sometimes in an unforeseen way! For example, having written the first movement of my Violin Concerto I quite unexpectedly abandoned going on with it until I had written the whole of the *Phyllida & Corydon* suite (35 minutes it takes to perform).
      All my love. Jack.
[Peers had now arrived back in England.]

November 25th   The Adelphi Hotel, Liverpool
My darling,
... The Liverpool hall seems acoustically perfect and it was wonderful to hear the sound of a good orchestra under such conditions. Bax's Third Symphony was magnificently played. It is a grand work, unfortunately not perfect — it has its lapses, but it has so much in it of such superlative beauty and grandeur as to atone for what might have been cut down ...
      All my love, Jack.

December 24th Kington
My darling,
I am very deeply immersed again at last in the 'cello concerto and have reached
the end of the expositionary section of the first movement ... I have re-written
the beginning part. There are now two extra bars in your first tune and two more
before you come in. From the point I have now reached onwards, it is going to
give me a lot of trouble. I see in my mind the shape of the whole movement, but
with me the process of working it out bar by bar on to paper is so terribly slow –
at least it is in this case, as it was with my Symphony, because I am putting into
it the best of which I am at the present capable. It is usually what sounds ultimately
the most spontaneous that actually is the most laboured in the making.
All my love and best Xmas wishes. Your Jack.

1945

January 13th The Adelphi Hotel, Liverpool
My darling,
... I have the whole of the string parts of the second and third movements of the
Sinfonietta to correct, and I find I must re-score the last three or four pages of
the finale entirely. After several days' experience of listening in Liverpool to a
full-sized orchestra in the flesh, not over the ether, I have learnt a certain point
of technique, namely that an important wood-wind passage as I now have it will
almost certainly be inaudible against a full body of strings such as I shall have
at Bedford with the B.B.C. Symphony Orchestra ...
All my love, dear Peers. Jack.

January 26th The Adelphi Hotel, Liverpool
My darling,
... I saw in last Monday's Telegraph that [Max] Rostal had something of an
ovation after repeating my [Violin] Concerto on Sunday last. I have since heard
that confirmed here in Liverpool since arriving here today. I shall have a lot to
discuss with you when I see you about our Concerto.
Meanwhile, I have just had a letter from Dublin to know whether I can have
it ready for you to broadcast in the Autumn at the Capital Theatre. Well, I can't:
it will take me longer to write it, apart from you learning it. Then, again, there
is the question of your playing it this side, preferably up here in Liverpool or
Manchester, where in both places you do get something more than a mere scrape
through by way of rehearsal.
Just fancy in London doing my Violin Concerto at the Royal Philharmonic
on one rehearsal for the whole concert. That is what they did. In London music
is in a state of decadence. There is no standard of artistic integrity: only box office

receipts are what count. As for the more 'advanced' or pseudo-serious aspects of music they have got into the hands of a small but powerful clique of left-wing politicians ... These are the people who in London hold sway in music. The Boosey and Hawkes projects are permeated with their propaganda: the L.P.O. under the auspices of Musical Culture Ltd. shelters bevies of these opportunists, who are making hay while the sun shines on better people than themselves serving their country.

I find myself here in Liverpool a kind of 'White-headed boy', and I feel all the more conscious that it is difficult to live up to it in the future with my appalling lack of technique and facility. What it boils down to, my darling, is this. I suppose I am appallingly selfish and I have certain dreams of what I want to do, but I can't do it unless I am in such an environment that I am able to work in peace.

Darling, forgive me for my being in a gloomy mood. These things have happened before, and I have always hitherto recovered my creative alertness.

I love you so much and, as you say, we may be wasting our time not being together, *Perhaps that is what is wrong.*

All my love, Jack.

January 27th   The Adelphi Hotel, Liverpool
My darling Peers,
... The concert is just over: the Symphony got a very hearty reception. Flash Harry [Sir Malcolm Sargent] and I had to come on several times. It was nice to hear it in the flesh under perfect acoustical conditions ...

Don't forget that in trying to settle down to work in London or in any big city at all is a very big experiment for me, whose whole musical and creative outlook for years past has been entirely bound up with the countryside ...

All my love, Jack.

January 28th
My darling Peers,
We had a wonderful concert today. Albert Sammons played a superb performance of the Elgar ... Earlier in the day I had a palaver with Albert S. over my Violin Concerto. Darling, he has been booked to play it with John Barbirolli for the Hallé tour in May! Anyway, he played the Elgar like someone inspired. He is, I am sure, just in a class apart as regards interpreting the kind of noises I perpetrate for the violin. I think that with the combination of J.B. and Sammons I shall really attain my ambition, i.e. to have my Concerto played just as I feel it.

I believe that you and I, you especially with your sympathy and help, will manage to produce a piece that goes perhaps more to the rock bottom of things than the Violin Concerto.

All my love. Jack.

135

February 8th   Kington.

Darling Peers,

… Yesterday and today I have been at work again on the Concerto and have been getting on well … the 'cello has been plugging away for sixty bars on end and now I am at a big climactic 'Tutt-eye' as I have sometimes heard it called − much easier to write than for your wretched instrument in combination with orchestra! The 'cello is the devil in this respect on account of its middle and bass register: frequently you must treat it as a solo, albeit alto or tenor part, and you must be careful not to put too much on top. Hence, I believe, the scarcity of 'cello Concertos owing to the technical difficulty in writing them.

All my love, darling Peers. Jack.

May 4th   Kington

My darling,

The present position is that from: −

I have inserted a return to the first subject, but in an entirely different way, consisting of 34 bars at the end of which we reach the key of F minor with you on top C after some brilliant passage work which I trust (but feel pretty sure) will be alright for the 'cello.

After this we lead into the new tune: −

in much the same way as before but a semitone higher. There are three reasons for what I have done after much pondering and reflection. (a) The question of form: the movement as it first was began to sprawl; moreover the very nature of the main subject seems to call for an insistance on the Rondo scheme. One is, I feel, fully justified in interpolating all sorts of tunes provided the movement is bound together by the main idea which in this case lends itself admirably to the purpose. (b) The tension wanted keeping up at this point with a longer lead up to the climax and more brilliant work for the soloist seemed called for before settling down for a time to be lyrical. (c) A change of key seemed essential with the climax and the new material which follows in the coming lyrical section.

136

The last interpolation in the Rondo was in E: –

Anyhow, I feel far happier about it now up to its present point. I had been getting very worried.

P.S. The Concerto is in a position which requires no more work today ... I am back in the tonic (in the major) after a section which contains probably what is best in the whole work and ends in soliloquy but the thing is how to round it off so as to make a satisfying ending. It will either require a little or a lot so far as I can see at present. It has got to be a brilliant finish: I have got back to the theme in quick 6/8 B major: – *

Anyhow, after some days sedentary I shall have to summon up energy to go up the hills and try and think out the finish.

[Jack and Peers were married on 26.7.45.]

October 1945   Ledbury

My darling,

Thanks for sending on letters, one was from Lionel Hill. I enclose a couple of photos. In the one in which I figure with him, had I not known it was myself I should have taken it for Albert Coates – the whole attitude and facial expression is that of A.C.!**

4.p.m. I have reached your entry: –

---

* This passage is actually in the key of E major in the published score.
** See page 55 in main text.

137

seven pages of score since breakfast.

I hope you won't mind my saying so, but I look upon the loss of edition one of the score as some special intervention of whatever guardian genius (or genie?) looks after me. All sorts of touches are in this new score that keep coming to me which were not in the old one. I was, as you know, unhappy about that last movement, and I suppose it was that I did not feel inspired scoring it as I seem to be this time. It is quite another thing to what the other would have been. If the other should turn up you will see the difference. Anyhow, I feel now that under present scoring conditions it is a good enough piece. I thought of a lovely bassoon thing this morning that wasn't there before and I am longing to see what other ideas crop up as I forge ahead. ... Goodbye darling for the present.

    Jack.

December 15th Kenmare
My darling Peers,
Your playing last night was just wonderful. I loved every minute of your performance. If anyone else wants to perform that work I won't let them have it! ... I gather that the whole of Kenmare tuned into you last night, and they all say what a wonderful wife I have! ...

    Love, Jack.

1946.

January 5th Kenmare
Darling,
You say you are cutting out smoking. I will reciprocate by going teetotal; it may be difficult, but I think it can be done.

Tomorrow, 12th day after Christmas, is the last day of our celebrations here. I may let fly with a few pints, but then I am definately going completely on the water waggon for at least a year ...

I had a letter from Mother today telling me about the Symphony. I now know that it was Clarence Raybould who conducted it. There is no mention whatever about it in the Radio Times. I do think somebody might have told me. It makes me depressed. These people who play one's music seem to have no thought that the composer might like to hear it — and it took me 2½ years to write. ...

    All my love. Jack.

January 7th Kenmare
Darling,
... The Eb Symphony progresses, but I am a bit stuck over the slow movement, also about the finish of the first. However, I have all the material for it and it will only be a matter of time working it out.

    All my love, darling Peers Jack.

May 5th   The New Inn, Rockland St. Mary, Nr. Norwich
My darling,
... Also, if you have it, send me Léon Goossens's address. I have now decided that the work will be a Quartet, definately not a Quintet, also I think I am getting the shape of it. Anyhow, I have more or less decided its opening. I want the week-end to let the general atmosphere of the place soak in.
        All my love. Jack.
[Jack is here referring to his *Fantasy Quartet* for oboe and strings, published 1947, and dedicated to Goossens.]

July 2nd   The Rectory. Ledbury
... Darling,
It is very enervating and airless here after East Anglia. Now I must get to work on doing a bit of writing out of the Quartet and also thoroughly mugging up the contents of my *Sinfonietta* score ...
        Love, Jack.

1947

May 30th   By the banks of the Blackwater. Kenmare
My darling,
... I have my music paper with me and have put in a couple of hours' composition out here in the sunshine. I can always work out my ideas best when out in the open. I think I have succeeded in writing some quite exceptionally (for me) good music this morning, and I hope to do some more after our picnic lunch. Re your letter, of course this holiday you speak about is quite necessary for you, and we will certainly go off together later on.

Apart from that, the Hills' offer is very kind. [We had offered them the use of our house while we were away on holiday. They eventually embraced this idea.]*

Please darling, try and take consolation from the fact that I am not being idle, and this trip is the birth of two more works, apart from the Symphony, one a movement for string orchestra (possibly à la Barber?), and the other a completely mad and wild Scherzo for orchestra. *Denny Island* is its title: this is a famous but lonely pub down the bay — famous for fiddling, melodeon playing and step-dancing in the kitchen. It has been closed for several years ... However, some ten days ago it re-opened in great style. I went over (a nice four-mile walk each way) for its re-christening, and I got the idea of this piece ... I think it may sound distinctly funny.

        Goodbye my darling. Your loving Jack.

---

* See page 72 in main text.

1948

March 8th   Kenmare
Darling,
I can't write very much because I am at the moment in a state almost amounting to stupor at the point I have reached in the Symphony. It may be imperfect in its present form but I think that in the last pages which complete the first section I have reached my high-water mark. It is rather luscious and Spring-like − or so I hope it will sound on the orchestra.

And incidentally, apart from the lovely Southern Spring here, your gorgeous 'cello playing which I listened-in to last week put me into such ecstasy that the next morning I really got going with a tune for 'cello, mostly in thirds and sixths. I've tried it out on one or two of the locals. I don't know whether they mean to be complimentary or not, but they say it reminds them of all the Kerry tunes put together.

The Symphony is taking a peculiar form.
All my love. Jack.

1949

[Peers is now in Australia]

February 5th
My darling Peers,
... The Dame is doing my Symphony at a B.B.C. symphony concert next Wednesday; of course this would just happen when you are scarcely out of the country, and I did so want you to hear it in the flesh. I have arranged to stay Tuesday night at Seer Green [with my wife and I]* and go up by the 8.10 a.m. Wednesday for rehearsal. The Carter broadcast my Trio last Monday and I am told the Oboe Quartet is in the Third programme week after next, so I am having a (temporary probably) spate of broadcasts of major works ...
Love. Jack.

February 6th   Ledbury. Airmail to Melbourne
My darling Peers,
... After writing last night I listened to Stravinsky's *Persephone* for tenor, chorus, orchestra and narrator. Here and there it was very fine, but a lot of it seemed pointlessly odd and inept.

---

* See p. 95 in main text.

140

February 7th Cheltenham. Airmail to Melbourne

Dear Peers,

This is a continuation of the other letter. I have had a week of hard work. There are now seven Irish folk-song settings; I sent a couple of them to Robert Irwin and he writes back that he hasn't been so excited for a long time and wants a whole set for a group in the Third programme.* Of the three which Sophie Wyss has she only appears to be singing one of them to any extent so that I have made her a copy of that one and sent it to her. She objected to one of them because it offended her Lutheran susceptibilities, being about the murder of a priest by 'heretics', and the other one, which is a lovely lament, slow and modal, I can tell the copy hasn't been much used, but the pretty-pretty one, *The Roving Dingle Boy*, she has sung all over Australia and elsewhere with success. It is, to me, the least attractive of the seven, rather the equivalent of *Nutting Time* in the Suffolk set. Some of them, too, have certain Irish words, and they really should be sung by an Irishman if possible.

I have today done for chorus one of the Suffolk ones; it has come out very nicely, really a lovely contrapuntal piece I think.** There is one more to do and then I shall turn to more serious work. As for hearing music, the Hungarians played Bartok No. 3 and the Franck Quartet. Really, there is some of the best of Franck in this work, but it is lacking in windows. Last night the Boyd Neel did Bach's *Ricercare* from the *Musical Offering*, I think this is one of the most wonderful short pieces of music ever written. Honegger's Symphony for strings followed ... it did not appeal to me. But then followed Strauss' *Metamorphosen* for twenty-odd solo stringed instruments, written in 1945. I had heard that the old man had perpetuated something unexpectedly fine in late life, but I was not prepared to be moved by the poignancy of this music, nor so spellbound by the dazzling meeting of counterpoint and richness, complexity and variety of texture.

We have had V–Williams' 6th Symphony twice this week. I am beginning to understand it a bit and to love it, but it is very frightening.

Love from Jack.

February 11th Cheltenham. Airmail to Melbourne

Darling Peers,

... As for my Symphony, Boult rose to the occasion and gave it a fine performance, really good. I heard he spent hours on it. So he did on Wednesday when I was there. He knew the score backwards and has his own ideas and suggestions and played it like he does Elgar. Basil Cameron wants to do the *Serenade* at Bath Festival in May.

---

* *Songs from County Kerry*, Augener, 1950.
** *The Jolly Carter*.

I stayed Tuesday night at Seer Green [at the author's house]. They are going on as usual. Betty is having treatment from Venables. [An osteopath recommended by Peers.]

All best wishes and love. Jack.*

February 16th   Cheltenham. Airmail to Melbourne
Darling Peers,
... Have been listening to a lovely Haydn Symphony No. 86 and Debussy's glorious *Iberia*. Also a new Stravinsky ballet suite, *Orpheus*. It struck one as lacking the choreography etc: hearing it in cold blood, but a very exciting part was beginning to materialize when I switched over to the Third programme to hear my Oboe Quartet.

Fondest love, Jack.

February 28th   Cheltenham. Airmail to Victoria. Australia
My darling Peers,
... I wondered, when you first told me, your plans of going to Australia en route to New Zealand, whether you might not find in the longer run that, from the point of view of being in the swim of music, Australia would not prove more alluring. You may end by going on to New Zealand for a certain time and returning to Australia, which seems to me to be really musically alive from what you say ... I wonder whether there may be some way of my getting out to Australia later on in some capacity or other. Do they like composers to conduct their own works? Anyway, I will write to Grainger and see what he suggests or perhaps can do when he gets to Australia in the Autumn. He is mad about the *Serenade* and keeps writing about it ...

A real musical thrill last night per wireless – Arnold Cooke of all people with a really masterly new Symphony. I had no idea he could be capable of such a really fine achievement.

All best love, Jack.

March 3rd   Cheltenham. Airmail to Melbourne
My darling Peers,
... I read that Stokowsky has just done my *In the Mountain Country* at New York Phil., my first orchestral work and published O.U.P. in 1925 ...

Love, Jack.

March 3rd   Cheltenham. Airmail to Melbourne
My darling Peers,
... If I come out later on I could teach composition and as for doing any conducting, you were present when I conducted here and, without boasting, I can

---

* See pp. 95–96 in main text.

tell you that the Cheltenham opinion was that, apart from Bliss, I was the best of the composer-conductors at the Festival ... Percy Grainger has written wanting to buy all my works and send them at his expense to Melbourne library.*

The Blech Quartet played Walton's Quartet here last night. It *is* a fine work.

All my love to you, Jack.

March 7th Cheltenham. Surface letter to Melbourne
My darling,

... I have been asked to adjudicate the compositions submitted for the Cheltenham competition festival in May − £12−12−0 fee, by no means to be sneezed at, and an interesting little job. I might spot a winner ...

What a nice fellow Maurice Miles is: he has made me the most generous offer any conductor has ever done. He said, 'Any time you have a new work and want to try out passages in it on the orchestra, bring it along and the Yorkshire Symphony Orchestra will be at your disposal'.

Love from Jack.

March 14th Cheltenham. Surface letter to Melbourne
My darling Peers,

... I am going for a long week-end to Seer Green [the Hills] on Friday evening; Lionel will take Saturday off ...**

I have been working again on the Symphony this evening.

My best love, Jack.

St. Patrick's Day
March 17th Cheltenham. Airmail to Melbourne
Darling Peers,

I listened in to the Trieste Trio last night. I was late in tuning in and it was not what the Radio Times advertised (Dvorak F minor) but it was obviously Dvorak. Afterwards the announcer said it was the Trio in E minor Op. 80. I looked it up in the book and found it was the one known as the Dumky Trio, which I always thought was hackneyed, but it seems I never could have heard it before. Still, I was 29 when I first heard and loved the Grieg Concerto.

I've heard from Lionel Hill to meet him tomorrow at Marylebone and travel down to Seer Green on the 5.15.***

Lots of love. Jack.

---

* The Grainger Museum has, in addition to many published scores of Moeran's music, the holograph full score of the *Serenade* (which includes the two movements omitted from the published version.

** See p. 95 in the main text.

*** See p. 95 in main text.

May 7th   Cheltenham

Darling Peers,

The climate here is unbearable this time of year. Cheltenham is noted for it.

I have just listened in to Fournier playing the Elgar — a remarkably fine and sensitive performance. This is more than I can say of Heifetz in the Violin Concerto at which I was present two days ago at Albert Hall. He certainly got through it in record time and made a disgraceful cut in the last movement, although he netted 1000 guineas! His playing was slick, efficient, brilliant and at times very Semitic. He did not play what Elgar wrote, frequently ignoring the composer's dynamics, tenutos and nuances. I was introduced to him by Albert [Sammons] at the rehearsal. He (Heifetz) says he has my Concerto under way, but is not ready with it yet.

Oh, my darling, how I do miss you and long for when we shall, I do hope, have a home together, one that we shall both be happy in.

All my love, Jack.

P.S. I think it an excellent idea for you to write to Harold Brooke [of Novello's]. Really, it makes me so depressed meeting foreign conductors who tell me they have wanted to do my works, but no material available. Van Beinum was the last one, referring to his own Concertgebouw Orchestra. It seems that apart from a few performances here the best that I have written in the prime of life i.e. Symphony, *Sinfonietta, Nocturne,* and the Concertos, 'Cello Sonata and songs, will just fizzle out and probably eventually go out of print and might as well never been written. Conversely, with my Overture, Joseph Williams has sent scores to about twenty conductors, and is lodging sets of parts out your way, in U.S.A. and elsewhere. Arthur Bliss, with the best intention, did a bad day's work for me when he introduced me to Novello's, e.g. as regards instrumental works. They are old-fashioned and half asleep.

About that suggestion for my coming to Australia in the New Year, I must, I am sadly afraid, wait until after the Festival here this time next year.

Love, Jack.

May 10th   Cheltenham

Darling Peers,

... I am sorry to say I am by no means satisfied with my Eb Symphony, well on towards the finish. I am terribly depressed about it as I fear it may have to be scrapped in toto.

All my love, Jack.

May 19th   Cheltenham. Airmail to New Zealand

My darling Peers,

... There is a proposition that I write the film music for a production of one of the Somerville-Ross stories. I shall know next week. The fee suggested is £500.

144

Darling, if it comes off I could come over to Australia, even if the first visit would be only a short one.

Love. Jack.

P.S. After my little change of air I feel happier about finishing the Eb Symphony.

May 25th Cheltenham

My darling,

... I am not being idle and, during being stuck with the Symphony, I am writing other things, madrigals etc: – you know, I think I am the only person in England if, being run in by the police, had to give my profession, could describe myself as 'Madrigalist'.*

May 27th Cheltenham

My own darling,

... Now I am going to undo a parcel containing the records of Albert's Norwich performance of my Violin Concerto, made from Lionel Hill's 'master' set. Mother had them made for me as an Easter present.

All my love. Jack.

May 31st

My darling Peers,

... I am hung up again with my Symphony so I am seriously considering your idea of trying to concoct another Quartet.

I had a letter from Boult today, in which he said he would play my works more often were he allowed to do so. I'm afraid he is a bit of a yes man, especially as he is reputed to have said at a luncheon party recently about me that I am not appreciated today, except by a minority of connoisseurs, but that in 25 years' time I shall be a household word. Then, if still alive, I shall be a coughing and rheumatic old half-wit of 79!

All my love, Jack.

June 14th Cheltenham

My darling,

Darling, the only thing that makes me hesitate about coming later and eventually to settle there with you is the older generation. My Mother has been so good to me for many years past, and she has this dread of my going away and never seeing her again.

I've got what may seem bad news for you. This Symphony which I started perpetrating in Eire and which I have been working on here simply will not stand.

---

* This would be *Candlemas Eve* (Herrick), Novello, 1950.

I had intended writing a work incorporating the four movements of a symphony into one, but I am conscious of the fact that I have failed, and I am not inclined to let go what I believe to be second-rate. I shall have to scrap this Symphony as it now is, nearly finished, and start afresh on something quite different.

As to the writing of it, the 'Venue' is wrong. If I were in Southern Ireland I could work it out and finish it, but it is absolutely and irreconcilably impossible to do it here. It started by being Irish, and if I try and put it right here, it only ends by being pastiche Irish. So it must go by the board. It's a pity, because the first part of the Symphony is so good, i.e. what I wrote in Ireland and shortly afterwards.

I would love to come and set up with you what I really do think we might make a happy home. Then, so far as I am concerned, I would write no more symphonies or concertos (unless I did another for you) but would devote my mellow years to writing chamber music and, I really think, on self-examination, that is the way I express myself best. Orchestrally, I am a bit of a fraud! I never mastered orchestral technique from A to Z, but I find I can never resist the impulse of being orchestrally brilliant, against my will sometimes.

Your own Jack.

P.S. We can't be separated for ever.

June 21st Cheltenham
My darling,
Well, darling, what you say about New Zealand is really beginning to make me keen about being there, apart from the natural propensity on my part to be with you always and forever so long as both of our lives last. I find I have little inclination to compose vast orchestral works any more. Honestly, I don't believe I have the technique. But I would love to write a lot more chamber music.

Of course, as you know well, the only snag ... is my Mother. I haven't the least urge to write anything for orchestra. It may be that I think that most conductors are showmen, frauds and charlatans, including J.B. who has been anything but a good friend over the Violin Concerto and its recording, either to Albert [Sammons] or to me.

July 26th Ledbury
Darling Peers,
This being our anniversary, I can't let the day pass without writing to send you my special love. This question of eventually migrating to the Antipodes on a permanent basis cannot be settled from this end. I am determined to get the Symphony written and produced at Cheltenham; incidentally, I had a good morning on it here, having written 30-odd bars before lunch.

I obviously can't go away any sooner. With regard to Norwich, 1951, and the

146

Festival of Britain, I told them I would write a work of a lighter nature, but could not possibly do another symphony still, which was asked for.

So they have given me absolute carte blanche.

Think it over darling.

All best love, Jack.

November 17th Ledbury. Airmail to Auckland. New Zealand,
to Peers from Jack' mother
[Jack is somewhere in Eire, suffering from severe drink problems.]
My dearest Peers,

Your letter to Graham [Jack's brother] just arrived. He will be writing soon. There is, at least, a little news of Jack. Graham had one letter, dictated to a friend, which said he was better, but his right hand useless for writing. When he does come home he will be told he must submit to definite treatment. We will do our very best to get him to the best place.

I am so sorry for you to have this continual worry. It is good to hear that you are having such a splendid success.

All my love to you. Mother

December 22nd Ledbury [Jack has returned home.]
My darling Peers,

... I may say that after the initial bout of drinking I got hold of a doctor in London, who put me on paraldehyde to make me sleep ... You know how sorry I am if I caused you anxiety, but I did not mean to do it.

Your very unhappy, Jack.

1950

January 14th—15th Ledbury
My dear Peers,

... How many more works would I have written if I had kept off the booze? My own opinion is that, as it is, I have written too many and would gladly scrap a lot that is in print, in fact practically all up to 1937, barring a few of the songs and the String Quartet.

There are two S.A.T.B. songs for the Fleet Street Choir (just published), a madrigal for male voices* and the seven Irish songs (in the press). That is all, except for the short score of the nearly complete Symphony of which, as you know,

---

* These songs were; *The Jolly Carter* (Suffolk folk-song) and *The Sailor and Young Nancy* (Norfolk folk-song). Both OUP, 1950.
The madrigal was *Candlemas Eve.*

I destroyed a lot and re-wrote, and now cannot make my mind up about, so much so that I have put it in abeyance as regards production. I ought not to have hung on in Cheltenham or any place that did not provide the immediate contact with nature.

I find myself disliking England more and more and if and when I get a clean bill of health I feel I would like to get right out of it and come away to where you are. Apart from all else I am being for ever pestered to write more orchestral works and, as I think I told you, my heart is not in it now nearly so much as in chamber music. But it will take a good many months before I know what medical opinion and my own judgement decrees.

January 29th   Ledbury
Darling Peers,
I went to London for two days and heard Beecham give a splendid performance of my *Sinfonietta* at a Royal Phil: concert, better than the previous one: he had, he told me, done it recently at Eastbourne. I was wired to come to discuss points of the score before rehearsal and Beecham came early to Albert Hall for the purpose; his score was full of his own markings which last time it was not, and he gave it far more rehearsal. After the concert he was very candid, asking me to send him scores of other works. I stayed with the Hills; they have sold Seer Green and taken a very quiet and roomy house in Brondesbury N.W.2 (4 Dawlish Road). They find it far more convenient and easier to run ...*

As for the Symphony, although I haven't actually committed any more to paper, I have spent a fair amount of time in thought over it, and I think I see daylight. But I really must have Irish surroundings and atmosphere where the beginnings sprang from ...
          Love, Peers dear, from Jack.

February 12th   125 Lower Baggot St. Dublin. Airmail to Melbourne
Darling Peers,
... I found my very old friend Larry Morrow ... He is a p.g. at a remote country cottage 17 miles out of Delgany, near the two Wicklow sugarloafs and 15 minutes' walk over fields to the sea ... It is ideal: the house full of books and culture ...
          Best love from Jack.

February 17th   125 Lower Baggot St. Dublin. Airmail to Melbourne
Darling Peers,
I have been going out again to Delgany and making arrangements with Sheila O'Mahony about furnishing of my room.

My work here has been research as to the origins of some of the Kerry songs

---

* See p. 101 in main text.

I am publishing and certain historical facts where I seem to have got garbled versions of names.

... Darling, it is so good to be in Dublin under sober conditions and am persevering with the treatment and I find I just don't feel the urge to consume drinks ... The very thought of whisky now revolts me.

Love from Jack.

February 25th   Ledbury
Darling Peers,
... In your letter of February 8th you say you might possibly do another New Zealand tour early in 1951, then South Africa with a view to making a trip home ... Schwartz* has written wanting to know if there is any chance of getting you for my Concerto and when. Also, Maurice Johnstone, musical director of B.B.C. Northern, doesn't propose engaging any other 'cellist for it pending your possible visit.

I, too, am saving money, now that I have cut out (and I hope this will continue) binges. If you do not come back, it is not easy to say quite when I could come owing to the necessity for getting works finished. I have postponed the production of the Symphony until Cheltenham 1951. Wilkinson thinks it better, as it will be part of the Festival of Britain.

My three weeks in Eire seem to have done me good as I now see what was wrong with it and I feel sure that in the lovely air, congenial home and beautiful scenary of Delgany, I shall forge right ahead.

The Third programme are doing the Beethoven Quartets. Op. 131 was superbly played. Surely it must be the greatest chamber work ever written.

February 28th   Ledbury. Armail to Melbourne
Darling Peers,
I have heard from Sheila O'Mahony; the address is: –

    Coolagad,
      Delgany,
        Co. Wicklow. Eire.

I hope to ensconce myself there during next week.

I may have to make a dash for Cambridge before I go back to Ireland in order to consult the University Library over one of the songs which I could not trace to its source in Dublin.

All my love, Jack.

---

* Conductor of the Bournemouth Municipal Orchestra. 1945–1951.

March 6th   In the train. Cambridge – London
Darling,
… I was at the Hills for the week-end and meet Lionel Hill at Albert Hall tonight to hear the Yorkshire Symphony Orchestra make their London début.*

I have had a lovely day in Cambridge; I tracked down and copied out the text of the Irish ballad I couldn't find in Dublin. I spent a pleasant hour with Patrick Hadley and Clifford Bax in Hadley's rooms. The other news is that Beecham appears to have been making a hit with my *Sinfonietta* and performing it elsewhere, in addition to the wonderful show he made of it at Albert Hall on January 25th. He wants all my scores so I have to see about this tomorrow.

Love again. Jack.

March 10th   125 Baggot Street. Dublin. Airmail to Sydney
Darling Peers,
I feel I must write you a short letter, my first night as a resident of Eire. I had a lovely crossing in perfect weather. The boat full of Welshmen coming over for the Ireland – Wales rugby match. As we steamed out of the Mersey river from Liverpool, they burst into song in perfect full-throated harmony as only the Welsh can put over in these islands: and there I stood on deck under a canopy of the lovely starlit Spring night listening to their music and quite entranced by it. I am staying the night in Dublin for tonight because I have to see Seumas O'Sullivan tomorrow morning re next year's Norwich Festival, having fixed-up with Hadley to set some of his poems for voice and orchestra for Parry Jones to sing.

All my love, Jack.

March 16th   Coolagad. Delgany. Co. Wicklow
Darling Peers,
… I have three works on the stocks (a) *The Oyle of Barley*, an orchestral fantasia on this tune from Playford, 1675, at the instigation of Barbirolli and Francis, Day and Hunter. It is going well and should be finished and off to the publishers by the end of this month. Then (April) I shall get back to the Symphony, on which I have put in two solid days this week to the end of a section.

I am working like blazes here in this lovely and peaceful place: also getting plenty of exercise walking and climbing.

Love from Jack.

March 20th   Coolagad. Co. Wicklow. Airmail to Melbourne
Darling Peers,
I got your March 8th letter setting out your reasons against making a trip to Europe. It is an awful long time to be parted. I must say I would like for us to

---

* See p. 102 in main text.

150

spend our old age somewhere round here, i.e. if we are both spared for a long life and if the world doesn't blow up.

So your sense of telepathy tells you I am not going on the bust. Actually, when I am really well and I hope normal (for me) I always, too, feel you closer to me and incidentally miss you an awful lot, so it is, in a sense, mutual – this feeling of one another's presence. By the way, you shouldn't talk about me taking a 'cure'; it is hardly that but simply that I take a medicine which has on my system the effect of making 'strong waters' repellant to me and I hope it will continue to work well. Mrs. L. says she has never seen me looking so well.

All my love, Jack.

[The next letter is the last extant to the woman he loved to the end of his life.]
March 20th Coolagad. Airmail to Melbourne
My darling,
Since writing a more practical and prosaic letter earlier today I have been out for a walk.

I just had to write you a few lines before post. After the wet week-end, everything is bursting out, lovely green shoots in the hedges, the purple heather on the mountain side, to the East the perfect blue of the sea. Darling, this makes me think the more of you and how you would love it. And here I am in this peaceful cottage in the thick of composition and finding things 'come easy' to me. There has been nothing like it for writing purposes since our happy time in Sussex.

Everything is perfect except that you are not here. I find that now I am working again amid the kind of country that is most dear to me, and living with kind people, sea, heather and mountains, that you, Peers, always seem to be not very far. Actually, I feel you with me when I am walking the hills. I love to think, and I believe and, in fact, know that you are with me spiritually, though so many miles separate us.

Goodbye, my own darling. With this lovely Spring, the birds singing, and everything day-by-day coming out (and I hope my music) you are always in my thoughts and I long to be with you again, and no more partings.

J.

[It is now known that no further work was done on the Symphony.]

Later in March, Jack visited specialists in Dublin, who warned him of pressure on the brain and/or severe heart trouble. He kept this news to himself, and began to indulge in bouts of heavy drinking. He left Delgany, never to return.

He turned up in Kenmare on June 16th 1950 and lived quietly and soberly until his death on 1st December.

Peers had no more letters from him after March.

* * * * *

A final revelation of the underlying tragedy that dogged Jack's creative life is revealed in the following letters, the first two of which were written to Peers by Jack's brother Graham:

September 3rd 1950   The Rectory. Ledbury. Airmail to Perth
Dear Peers,
I knew that Mother had told you all that we had heard about Jack, which was very little. I have written to Sheila O'Mahony three times ... and had two replies – very nice and kind but not awfully helpful ... I offered to go over to Eire if it was thought to be any use for me to do so, but Miss O'Mahony said she felt it wouldn't be. She will do her best, if Jack can be found, to persuade him to undergo psychological treatment under an excellant doctor they know of ... but he has first got to be found and then agree to this – you can't *force* a man of his age to undergo treatment unless he is willing. That's the only stumbling block – but its a big one ... Of course if we get any definate news we will let you know at once. I am so sorry for you in all your anxiety. The prolonged silence is proving a great strain on poor Mother.
        Love from Graham.

December 6th   [Six days after Jack's death.]
        At Glenview Hotel. Delgany. Airmail to Victoria
My dear Peers,
I am using for this letter an air-letter with stamp attached already which was among poor Jack's few belongings at Kenmare, clearly indicating that he had intended writing to you. But it seems he couldn't concentrate for long together. So far as I can guage, the only letter which he wrote during the whole time of his uninterrupted sojourn at Kenmare from June 16th until the day he died was the one to Mother which I referred to in my previous letter, and which, I believe, he was prompted to write by Mrs. O'Donnell. [Jack's landlady.] In it he said that his lucid moments were very limited and that his main dread was that he would be certified insane and shut up in an asylum. Your last letter to him, dated October 24th, was taken from one of his pockets after he was dead ...
    From what Sheila told me last night, Jack was alright – or pretty well so – until a day when a specialist examined his eyes in Dublin and advised him to see another specialist. Then, we imagine he was warned in some way of the danger of something pressing on his brain, or of the state of his heart, but the nature of which he confided to no one; at any rate, from then until he left Coolagad, he drank heavily – went away, sent a message that he'd been robbed, and disappeared until the middle of June, when he turned up at Kenmare.
    During Jack's sojourn at Kenmare, it appears that he lived very quietly and soberly since the end of June. He pottered about, listened to the wireless, gave

152

a child he was interested in some music lessons, played the piano to his friends — but that was all. His days of work were over, owing pretty certainly to some head injury and his heart not in a good state. It was far better, therefore, that he should pass on now than linger — maybe for years — becoming more childish. So that should cheer you, as it does me.

Love from Graham.

December 10th   The following airmail was from Mrs Varley, Peers' sister
Coombe Cottage. Lyme Regis
Darling Peers,
I hope before you get this that you have had Graham's letters and cables. I had the opportunity to meet him on my way here yesterday. Mrs Moeran is suffering from delayed shock and it was thought wise to keep her very quiet. I was glad to have Graham's account of everything. He talked for about two hours with all the loving sympathy one could wish for.

Jack died, rather as he would have wished, looking out on the waters of Kenmare bay, which he loved so much. I can so understand that vagueness which descended on him preliminary to a stroke. I have seen the same thing happen to Mummy. It makes it impossible for them to concentrate sufficiently to write a letter. She has sometimes asked me if I thought she was going out of her mind and that was Jack's fear too. I hope you can take some comfort from this and realize why Jack didn't write. Although I scarcely knew Jack, I do truly grieve for him dying in loneliness and without hope of seeing you again. He had your last letter in his pocket when he died and you did mean so much to him, and I grieve for you knowing this to be true and not an overdrawn picture.

To cure his incurable disease was beyond his own power even for your sake, and *that* you should have both faced up to before marriage. To keep it at bay would have been a continual battle for both of you and I think you, as well as his family, were ignorant of the medical facts.

I wish I could help in some way, but I really think no good purpose would be served by your coming back just now. You must tell me if I can do anything in your stead.

Much love, Sheila.

[In 1984 the afore-mentioned Mrs Sheila Varley, Peers' sister, wrote two letters to the author, from which the following extracts have been taken: —]

8th August   4 Timberleaze. Gastard. Wiltshire
Dear Mr. Hill,
... I scarcely knew Jack — I met him once before he married Peers; I was present at the ceremony and once he came to see us when my son was very young. He

that Peers was soon disenchanted with the marriage and how long they were actually together I don't know. His parents were alive when he married and they were delighted about it. Old Mrs. Moeran treated Peers as a daughter. They said 'Jack has a tendency to drink'. They did not know how awful it was, for at the end of every bout lasting about three months, he always returned to Mother in a dreadful state and she always welcomed him home. They thought that marriage would be the cure. Just about the time of the wedding the family doctor [Dick Jobson] wrote Peers a letter which made her very angry. He said that she must only expect brief periods of happiness with Jack.

Peers honestly didn't know about alcoholism − she didn't know that there was such an incurable disease. I had read about it and knew that the only hope was to have no drink in the house and no drinking parties etc. She only spoke of what she went through, and she was horrified at the reality before she went to Australia and went off saying that she would make a home for him if he was cured. After the honeymoon she threw one of her usual parties and of course started him off on a bout.

He wanted her to live with him in a cottage in Kenmare but it wouldn't have suited the career of an active musician. He would have been away from those hard-drinking friends of his.

We always had a feeling that he didn't really want to get married; after all, he was fifty and she was forty when they did.

September 24th
Dear Mr. Hill,
... Peers was a strange mixture − genuinely ignorant of some aspects of life, insensitive to people's needs, but loving. She must have had pretty poor judgement, for in planning her life with Jack (if she ever seriously did so) she must have known the requirements for a composer, and seemed genuinely surprised that he needed a separate studio. He had always had ideal conditions for his work at home ... She was greatly flattered that music should be written for her to play, and told Jack that she wouldn't marry him till he had finished the Concerto.

Someone − it must have been my Mother − said that she thought that though Jack loved Peers he didn't really want to marry anyone.

The old Moerans had so little knowledge of the disease that they called it 'a tendency to drink' and thought that marriage would cure that. Peers had very horrific experiences of this drink problem in London which she told me about. Once he started he would go on for three months.

You gave a true picture of his last months.

Graham guessed that the specialist had diagnosed a serious physical condition and may have even said he hadn't much longer to live. He certainly had a fear of madness. Graham managed to suppress any mention of what he found in Jack's pockets. There were chains and padlocks. He had an idea that he would be taken away to an asylum and meant to chain himself to something to prevent it. Apparently if you are going to have a massive stroke you feel very strange for some time beforehand.

P.S. I have written on a very personal note ...

Yours sincerely,
Sheila Varley

* * * * *

Thus it was that this shy, lovable and gifted man was cursed by an incurable disease, aggravated by wounds suffered in the First World War. We can only marvel at, and be grateful for, the consistantly high level of his musical output, the poetic integrity of which will not fade in the years to come.

Appendix 'C'
Current discography

ORCHESTRAL

Symphony in G minor	Halle, Heward (rec. 1942)	
	mono (2 recs)	EM290462-3
		EM 280462-5
	English Sinfonia, Dilkes	ED290187-1
		ED290187-4
	New Philharmonia, Boult	SRCS70
Violin Concerto	Georgiadis, LSO, Handley	SRCS105
Cello Concerto	Coetmore, LPO, Boult	SRCS43
	Wallfisch, Bournemouth Sin-	Chandos
	fonietta, Del Mar	(1986 release)
Rhapsody No. 3 in F sharp, for piano and orchestra		
	McCabe, New Philharmonia,	SRCS91
	Braithwaite	
Sinfonietta	LPO, Boult	SRCS37
	Bournemouth Sinfonietta,	Chandos
	Del Mar	(1986 release)
Rhapsody No. 2	LPO, Boult	SRCS43
Lonely Waters; Whythorne's Shadow		
	English Sinfonia, Dilkes	ESD7101
		TC-ESD7101
	(*Lonely Waters* only)	TC2-MOM104
	(with Symphony)	ED290187-1
		ED290187-4
Overture to a Masque	LPO, Boult	SRCS43

CHAMBER AND INSTRUMENTAL MUSIC

String Trio in G	Members of Hanson String	SHE563
	Quartet	
Fantasy Quartet for oboe and strings		
	Sarah Francis, English Quartet	ABRD1114
		ABTD1114
	John Anderson, Thamyse Trio	AIR2-9005
Cello Sonata	Peers Coetmore, Eric Parkin	SRCS42
Prelude for Cello and Piano		
	Peers Coetmore, Eric Parkin	SRCS42

Stalham River; *The White Mountain*;
Toccata; *Prelude and Berceuse*; *Bank Holiday*;
Two Legends (*A Folk Story* and *Rune*)

	Eric Parkin		SRCS42
Bank Holiday	John McCabe	on	SDD444
Three Fancies	Eric Parkin	on	BDRD2006
			(2 recs)
		on	DBTD2006

SONGS

Ludlow Town — song cycle (Housman)

	Graham Trew, Roger Vignoles		E77031-2

Far in a western brookland;
'Tis time, I think, by Wenlock town (Housman)

	Graham Trew, Roger Vignoles	on	E77031-2

The Bean Flower;
Impromptu in March;
Four English Lyrics

	Anne Dawson, Roderick Barrand		A66103

Four Shakespeare Songs
(1. *The lover and his lass*; 2. *Where the bee sucks*; 3. *When daisies pied*;
4. *When icicles hang by the wall*)

1—4	Alfreda Hodgson, Keith Swallow		SHE559
2—4	Graham Trew, Roger Vignoles		A66026
In Youth is pleasure	Peter Pears, Benjamin Britten	on	ECS545

The Merry Month of May

	Peter Pears, Benjamin Britten	on	ZRG5439

RECORDINGS IN THE BBC SOUND ARCHIVE

A Seaman's Life: Stanley Riley (bass) and BBC Men's Chorus (19/10/42).
East Anglia Sings: a programme of folksongs recorded in Norfolk and
    Suffolk. E J Moeran, recordist and speaker (7/11/47).
Down by the Riverside (rec. 16/8/49).
Spring the Sweet Spring (15/12/50).
Strings in the Earth and Air (16/8/49).
Irish Love Song: Havelock Nelson, piano (11/8/60).
The Merry Month of May: Peter Pears and Benjamin Britten (22/6/65).
Seven Poems of James Joyce: Patricia Joyce and Wilfred Parry (4/6/71).
Oxford May Morning Carols: Magdalen College Choir, conductor Bernard Rose
    (1/5/72)
Vocal settings of James Joyce: Meriel Dickinson and Peter Dickinson (17/10/72).

Appendix 'D'
Principal works

ORCHESTRAL

In the Mountain Country (1921)
Rhapsodies Nos 1 and 2 (1924)
Whythorne's Shadow (1931)
Lonely Waters (1932)
Suite: Farrago (1932)
Symphony in G minor (1934–7)
Violin Concerto (1942)
Overture for a Masque (1944)
Sinfonietta (1944)
Cello Concerto (1945)
Rhapsody, for piano and orchestra (1945)
Serenade in G (1948)

CHAMBER MUSIC

Trio, for violin, cello and piano (1920)
String Quartet in A minor (1921)
Sonata for 2 unaccompanied violins (1930)
Trio, for violin, viola and cello (1931)
Violin Sonata (1935)
Phantasy Quartet, for oboe and strings (1946)
Cello Sonata (1947)
Prelude, for cello and piano (1944)
Irish Lament, for cello and piano (1952)
String Quartet in Eb (1956)

SONGS

Ludlow Town (1920)
Seven Poems by James Joyce (1930)
Four English Lyrics (1934)
Four Shakespeare Songs (1940)
Six Poems by Seamus O'Sullivan (1944)

FOLK-SONGS ARRANGEMENTS

Suffolk Folk-Songs (6)
Norfolk Folk-Songs (6)
Songs from County Kerry (7)

CHURCH MUSIC

Praise the Lord, O Jerusalem (1930)
Te Deum and Jubilate (1930)
Magnificat and Nunc Dimittis in D (1931)
Blessed are those servants (1938)

CHORAL

Songs of Springtime (1933)
Nocturne (1934)
Phyllida and Corydon (1939)

PIANO SOLO

Three Pieces (1919)
Theme and Variations (1920)
On a May morning (1921)
Stalham River (1921)
Toccata (1921)
3 Fancies (1922)
2 Legends (1923)
Bank Holiday (1925)
Summer Valley (1925)
An Irish Love Song (1926)
The White Mountain (1927)
Prelude and Berceuse (1933)

158

Index